WRITE THAT BOOK NOW

On getting books written and life lived

PHILIP J BRADBURY

Published by: The Write Site, Brisbane, Australia
ISBN- 978-0-6485021-1-1

Copyright 2020 © Philip J Bradbury

Philip J Bradbury has asserted his right under the Copyright, Designs and Patents Act 1988 to be identified as the author.

All rights reserved. No part of this publication may be reproduced or transmitted in any form or by any means, electronic or mechanical, including photocopying, recording or any information storage and retrieval system, without permission in writing from the publisher.

❦❦❦   ❧❧❧

Other books by Philip J Bradbury

Non-Fiction
Life Rejuvenated
Whose Life Is It Anyway?
Change Your Life, Change Your World
The Twelve Week Miracle (with Anna Bradbury)
Conversations On Your Business
How To Get Out of Debt ... and stay out forever

Some-Fiction
53 SMILES
97 SMILES
Dactionary - a dictionary with attitude
45 Moments With Men

Fiction
The Last Stand Down
My Whispering Teachers
Circles of Gold
Gerald the Great of Gorokoland
The Meaning of Larf

For more information on these books, see
www.philipjbradbury.com

My ripping pen

Amid the Forest of Confusion I staggered. Panicked. Was overwhelmed. Finally, I stopped struggling, leaned against a doorway and beseeched her help. I immediately saw the benign half-smile of the Strumpet of Writing before me. Her gentle fist smashed into my face and I crumpled like jelly-beans, released from their bag.

For aeons I avoided writing, projected my pain and pretended I was coping. But I coped less and less, falling further and further each passing day. Eventually, at the bottom of the abyss, I collapsed from the weight of life, kneeling on the floor with the red pill in my quaking fingers, ready to end it all. One final, plaintive entreaty and a gnarled finger gently lifted my chin to look upon the benign half-smile of the Denizen of Writing.

"Take your pain, Dear One," he said. "Hold it gently, reverently, gracefully, and let it be your muse."

The pill became the pen and, with it, I stabbed my pen to the white, virgin page, the pen red and dripping.

I took not the writing up but let it take me up. It came not from me but through me.

I became the grateful observer while the pen became the steersman and my pain and anguish the wind that filled my sails. It blew in hurricanes and breezes, in tornadoes and zephyrs and, puff by ragged puff, drip by bloody drip, my pain eased from me, through the words and I released myself into my books.

The pages lost their virginity and I lost my grief and smile again.

Philip J Bradbury

For more books from Philip J Bradbury, use your phone to scan this QR Code - you'll be taken to my website at
https://philipjbradbury.com

Contents

Welcome	9
A snapshot of what you're in for	
Why This Book	13
What's the point of reading this?	
Why Do I Write?	16
Whence Our Ideas?	17
I want to write but I don't know what to write about	
Flying, Writing & Being Off Course	21
I try to move ahead but I keep going off course	
Contaminative Proximity & Clarity	23
You have a choice every moment. Choose your own truth.	
You Might be a Writer if …	27
Are you mad or just a writer?	
Writing is not Homeopathy	29
The sport of finding your own voice	
Beware The Writing Police	32
I don't know the writing rules so I'm not a good writer	
Storytelling Rules	35
My English isn't good and I don't know the rules of writing	
Communicating to Confuse	40
I'm not sure if I can explain things clearly	
Turn Up At The page	42
I don't have time to write a novel	
Writing On Empty	44
I always get writer's block. I keep getting stuck.	

For more courses, resources and forces to help you write your book use your phone to scan this QR Code - you'll be taken to my website at
https://writethatbooknow.com

Create Spaces	48
I never get in the mood for writing, though I want to	
Writers Block and the Kaleidoscope Life	51
What if I can't make myself write or I can't think of anything?	
The Bitch On Your Shoulder	55
I'm too critical of myself to take the risk	
A Gardener Tidies His Garden	57
Keeping myself going by making my progress public	
I Am Such a Perfectionist	60
I'll never let my book be finished	
I'm a Procrastinator	64
I'm good at starting projects but not finishing them	
Aiming for One Thing, Getting Something Else	67
I never seem to achieve my goals	
Persistence	69
There is so much competition, I won't succeed	
The Persistence Of Paulo Coelho	73
The story of a story-man who didn't give up	
Walking My Talk and Remembering	76
I keep regretting my inaction but still can't get going	
Questions Are More Powerful Than Answers	80
How do I conquer writer's block?	
Why Do I Choose Failure?	83
I give up easily – how do I keep going?	
Apple Cider, Doing It Badly And Writing	85
I keep being diverted by things – how do I stay on track?	
Creative Spaces	89
I can't write where and when others tell me to	

Accepting Judgement   92
 I don't think I can deal with the criticism I'll get for my book
Wisdom And Words From The Silence   94
 Most of us listen to the outer world and it's not always nice
Isolation And Interaction – Writers Groups   99
 I don't know any other writers and I need support
Confessions of a Magazine Writer   102
 Persistence, bloody persistence and unexpected magic
Are We There Yet?   106
 I love writing but I don't want to write a whole book.
How Long Should My Book Be?   108
 ... and other writing facts
Story Structure and Characters   110
 Which parts of the story comes first, second and so on?
FOR PLANNERS   114
Why Are You Writing This book?   116
 What bugs you?
Why Are You Writing This book?   118
 Where have you been?
Why This Book?   120
 Matching passions with experiences
What Is The Point Of Your Story?   121
 The ONE BIG THING
Ordering Thoughts And Emotions   123
 Unjumbling the jumble
Words Are But Symbols of Symbols   126
 I don't know how to explain intangible things.
Ambidextrous Writing   128
 Answers to all my questions
About the Author   130
 Social media

Writing is a most peculiar sport: a solitary activity to create a public spectacle.

It's definitely not a team sport and our only companions are a pen, a pad and the untameable mystery of that which brings words – memory, imagination and something else ineffable. From this intangible mystery we are to conceive and give birth to a very tangible tribe of words who scream to the world for attention.

Within this there are two challenges:

1. There is no single formula for which words to write and in what order. We are left totally on our own and it's only afterwards, when 100,000 words have been lovingly etched onto paper or screen that other people will arrive to pull them apart.

2. To play this solitary sport, one must be a solitary-seeker; at least for a time … a long time. Comfortable in our own space we must, then, step into the space of least comfort and expose our fragile new children to the world. We must bare our solitary souls, defenceless against the jibes, compliments and indifference we might encounter.

Yes, writing is a most peculiar sport and here is one writer's kind guidance to playing a safer, more supported game for you.

Welcome

A snapshot of what you're in for

Welcome to *Write That Book Now*. I am Philip J Bradbury, your slave driver ... aaah, I mean I am your writing coach!

So, quickly, a little about the book, a little about me and a small introduction to writing ...

About the book/course
This book/course is for you if you:
- If you have started your book and you've become stuck, for some reason,
- If you have a story or a theme you want to write about but haven't started for whatever reason, or
- If you really want to write but you can't think what to write about ... or how to start.

Whatever stage you're at, this book will help you get your story – or any other writing – written, whether you want it published, if it's just for close family or if it's simply for your own healing and/or peace of mind.

You won't learn about graphic design, printing, publishing, marketing or any of the things you need to do after you've written the words - that's in a subsequent course.

Step one is to get the words on paper and that's a big enough task in itself.

About me

I have written 18 self-published books so I've been getting my books written! I have also edited, designed and published over fifteen books for other authors and you can see some of them on my website at www.philipjbradbury.com.

I've been a magazine columnist, editor and publisher at different times and in different parts of the world, as well as a freelance writer for clients round the globe.

Right now, I'm working with a team to turn one of my novels into a podcast and then (hopefully) into a movie. I'm also engrossed in writing my Great Australian Novel and doing this, partly, through a writing course in which I am a student. We never stop learning and it definitely helps to have the support of others to keep me on track and to see the bumps in the road that I don't.

I write every day – 500-2,000 words a day – and will continue writing even if none of my words were ever published. I just love the process, the creativity and the otherworldliness I can plant into each and every day of my life. For example, I just wrote the 936 words of this Welcome chapter in 40 minutes this morning.

I do my best to walk my talk and I won't ask you to anything I haven't done or won't do. In a sense, we are doing this course together.

So that's a snapshot of my writing.

About writing

As a trainer/life coach for over 25 years, I take the view that there are universal laws and techniques to take us to where we want to be. Writing a book, in many ways, is the same as any other endeavour, including the biggest endeavour … your life!

You will learn these laws and techniques through this course.

However, at the same time, writing takes particular and unique skills that some are born with, some can learn and some will never acquire. Writing is beset with so many rules and, at the same time, is an art. As an art, it is an open invitation to breaking rules!

Writing is, for example, not like brain surgery. If we make a mistake we can erase and rewrite. Our errors are seldom life-threatening! Also, a brain surgeon's career may improve the lives of hundreds of people whereas your book may touch millions of people in unexpected ways. For example, I've had messages from people who decided not to commit suicide and decided not to abandon their marriages after reading my words.

However, like the brain surgeon, we need to learn our craft, to practise our craft, to practise our craft, to practise our craft … and keep practising our craft.

Malcolm Gladwell tells us in his book, *The Outliers*, that success only comes after 10,000 hours of practicing our craft and he uses The Beatles, Bill Gates and many others as his examples. This 10,000-hour rule may or may not apply to you but if you think you can learn a few tips and whip up a book in the next month, you have no business in this career, in this activity or with this book.

Melissa Ashley, who is running the course I am doing, has had two books published. She rewrote her second book four times before her agent – and her, eventually – was happy with it.

Writing is a marathon and requires constancy, regularity and discipline.

"What? Discipline?" I hear you exclaim. "But art and discipline don't go together!"

"Oh yes they do," I reply.

The artform itself may reject discipline and rules but you've got to turn up to your blank canvas, blank page or unchipped stone in order to enjoy your art. And turning up may require rearranging your schedule or your family's schedule. It may require giving up current activities to enjoy your art. This requires discipline and planning.

Also, your book will probably require some planning; more so if you're a planner than if you're a pantser - words we'll describe soon.

This course will cover all aspects of creative writing, not academic writing. There are exercises at the end and, today, your mission is to answer five questions for yourself:
1. Why do I want to write?
2. Why am I writing?
3. Who do I want to write for?
4. How will my writing help/affect my readers?
5. How will it affect me?
6. On a scale of one to ten, how committed and passionate are you about finishing this book of yours?

Turn to the last section – Why are you writing this book? – and you can answer these questions.

Why This Book

What's the point of reading this?

This book/course is about getting your book written. It is not about getting it published. We can help you with the publishing later but let's focus on one thing at a time ... one big thing at a time.

Writing a book is a big project and let's not pretend otherwise. And publishing and marketing are another big project. Thinking and worrying about two big things is too much for most brains and that's why so many good writers give up and why so many good stories are stillborn ... or aren't even conceived.

Do one thing today – write. And tomorrow – write. And the next day – write. That, for now, is your mission and we'll help you get that book written, day by day by day. That's enough to focus on right now.

So, a quick introduction to writing and writers:
There are two types of writers – pantsers and planners. Hence, there are two sections to this book – the first for pantsers and the second for planners.

Pantsers, like Stephen King, fly by the seat of their pants. Hence the name, pantsers. They sit down, each day, with the intention to get out of their own way, to be surprised and to see what is going to happen on the blank page. They usually have no idea how the story is going to end, despite continually wondering what it might be.

Planners, like John Grisham, plan their whole novel long before they start writing. They might set up storyboards or vision-boards for each chapter, mapping out every scene. They know where the story starts and finishes, who all the characters are and, only after they've built that detailed, predetermined structure, will they then start writing the story. It might not come out as planned but there's a firm intention and a plan every step of the way.

Both John Grisham and Stephen King are successful writers and no method is better than another. It simply depends on the type of person and my advice is ...

Do. Not. Obey. Other. People. Telling. You. How. To. Write. Got that? Listen to them and then make your own mind up.

You're made the way you're made and to try and fit into something that doesn't fit just gives you headaches, insomnia, exasperation and you'll likely give up. Do not give up. Do not stop being yourself, with all the quirky weirdness that makes you what you are.

Some writers like writing in busy cafés (like me), some take themselves off to wilderness retreats, some like writing with herds of other writers – like the NANOWRIMO movement – and some ... well, there's an endless list of suitable environments.

Stephen King has a rigid daily routine that starts at 4.30 am with writing, breakfast, dog-walking, writing and he stops before lunch.

Paulo Cuelho writes for 24 hours a day, for two weeks a year, and then he has 50 weeks a year to travel and research.

James Paterson churns out so many books because he has a team of ten writers and he exercises editorial control.

David Gaughan, writer of *The Blue Star* (that I published), wrote his 80,000 words between midnight and 4.00 am, every morning, over three months.

There's an unlimited number of routines so play with

different ideas, schedules, places and times till you find your preferred method.

There. Is. No. One. Way. To. Write.

Find your own rhythm, environment, drugs, therapist, tribe and system and just get on and write in the way that comes most comfortably for you.

There are, of course, many shades of grey between planners and pantsers so you're not necessarily one or the other. Because you're likely to be a unique hybrid, somewhere between the panster and planner, this book is designed with techniques, exercises and ideas for all writers on the continuum. You'll find something in here, wherever you stand on the spectrum.

The lesson is to honour yourself, quirks and all.

Why Do I Write?

Looking for recognition, looking for acceptance,
Not knowing where to find them,
Or even what they look like,
Stumbling and plodding in relentless pursuit.

Like a marksman firing at a target never seen,
Fire enough rounds, something will connect.
Like a blind man in a zoo, hands through a hole,
Hoping it's the ticket office, not the lion's cage.

People constantly remind me that my books aren't selling,
And suggest I return to money-making prison,
Not knowing the freedom I feel inside,
With words sculptured, massaged and nurtured.

For those without a passion or sense of destiny,
It's hard to imagine doing something,
With no certainty of profit or success,
A selfish, self-indulgent and impractical pursuit.

So I write and I write and I write.
Another café, another tall story,
I write as it fills, as it trills,
No reason. No reason beyond a smile.

WHENCE OUR IDEAS?

I want to write but I don't know what to write about

People ask writers how they come up with their stories, how they pluck characters and stories from thin air, how the ideas come to them. I can't speak for other writers and I really have no idea how the ideas, plots, people and places bring themselves together for my pen to describe. However, I don't how a car works but know what I need to do to make it work. Similarly, I know what I need to do to have the writing happen – here are some of those things

1. Get out of your own way

We know not whence our ideas come from.

"Ripple on still waters, where there is no pebble tossed, nor wind to blow," wrote and sang Gerry Garcia of The Grateful Dead. The ripples (ideas) come when there is nothing to disturb them.

I know that the ideas come when I still my mind, when I let the world, its disturbances and expectations go ... when my pond is left to settle, to be still and smooth.

That is when my ideas come.

And then my mind gets in the way and asks – how did I think that? Where did that thought come from? Why am I thinking this? What should I write next? – the thoughts tail off.

And when I judge – that's weird, what a silly idea, that's a great idea – they tail off.

Left to themselves – unquestioned and unjudged – they flow through my pen and go where I could not expect.

It's worth pond-ering, don't you think!

2. Focus

When you've heard the call from the depths of your soul – the call that is illogical, fearful and breathtakingly beautiful – you'll find your focus shift to possibilities with words or whatever your soul is calling you to do.

I have a friend, Darryl, who builds stretched limousines. He's done it for many years and has stretched every type of vehicle imaginable. He's passionate about his amazing creations and his mind is constantly on the lookout for new and interesting ideas. Whether he's in a shop, a house, a train or anywhere else, he's constantly scouring door knobs, windows, shapes, colours, technology and every other thing that comes to his five senses, to be adapted to his next project. Because of his focus, he's never short of ideas – they just seem to jump out at him in ways we can't imagine.

Similarly, a writer is constantly scanning their world for sights, sounds, smells, feelings and ideas that can be turned into an interesting string of words. In fact, this chapter was inspired by one of my students who suddenly discovered that I have a life outside the university lecture room, a secret life of writing. She asked me, "So, how do you find things to write about?" Most other people would do little with such a comment but it has spurned over 2,000 words from me. That's what focus does – it takes the banal, the ordinary, the commonplace, and turns it into something creative.

Comedians are able to observe the same world as you and I and turn that into something funny, in ways you and I can't. Similarly, writers take what most people see as rubbish and turn it into fertilizer for their next word-project.

This consistent focus, this constant search, may seem like

hard work. It's not hard work at all. For Darryl, there is nothing so enjoyable as finding several new ideas and then going to the drawing board in his mind – or the one in his workshop – and tinkering and calculating and adjusting and experimenting and, eventually, coming up with something more beautiful, clever and/or practical than anyone else has ever created before.

For me it's fun. I enjoy hearing comments and/or learning different things that have no apparent relationship to each other and then putting them together in ways no one else has thought of. It's also more than fun. It's become so natural I sometimes catch myself doing it and then realise I've been doing it all along, without conscious awareness. It becomes effortless, natural and constant.

I am continually amazed that soap-opera writers can create new episodes, every day, on TV and they never repeat themselves – a never-ending supply of events and dramas. Or song-writers who churn out song after song. Creating their episodes and songs may seem like hard work – and it is sometimes – but they are so focused on their passion, their constant focus has the episodes and songs popping out of thin air.

Both Lionel Richie and Michael Jackson committed themselves to writing a song every day for a year. They didn't know each other at the time and, coincidentally, made the same commitment to themselves – they wouldn't allow themselves any breakfast until they had finished each day's song. Obviously, a part of this is Rule # I – Turning Up At The Page . From 365 songs, some of them had to be winners! Also, completing a daily project, every single day, is hugely satisfying. The work involved is linked with the satisfaction of completion … and then work becomes identified with satisfaction, not unpleasantness. They transferred the act of song-writing from one of hard, unrelenting work into one of sheer pleasure and, after a year of that, neither wanted to stop the pleasure … and neither did.

So, the news of the day, ladies and gentlemen, is that focus can seem like hard work – and it sometimes is – but as we practise it, as we exercise our focus muscle, it becomes easier and more pleasurable. Eventually, it becomes automatic and we don't want to stop.

The other news, ladies and gentlemen, is this: if what we're doing comes from the deepest, most peaceful part of our being, it comes to us as gently as a butterfly landing on our shoulder. That gentle landing onto the place of our passion and peace can only come when we give ourselves permission to do so ... which is the subject of the next chapter.

3. What annoys you?

So, what comes up from the deepest, most peaceful part of your being?

Weirdly, it is likely to be something very un-peaceful! Think about the thing that most annoys you. That which really upsets you. That which constantly niggles at you ... what, in this illogical, insane, abusive and destructive world really gets on your craw?

Often, the answer comes from your childhood. Did you feel you weren't listened to, were abused, were belittled were ... whatever? Even with perfect parents, friends and teachers, everyone still dredges up and carries aloft some grievance.

Maybe it's abuse of woman, of the environment, of children, of men, of money, of – yes, the list can go on and on.

So, think about:
- What you mainly complain about,
- Of all the dramas in the world, which ones seem to gleefully follow you, day after day.

That Point of Pain – yes, we all have one – can trigger your most passionate, transcendent and translucent writing.

So, still yourself, observe what you focus on and what bothers you. That is your starting point – you!

Flying, Writing & Being Off Course

I try to move ahead but I keep going off course

Have you ever noticed that aeroplanes don't always take off in the direction they want to go? They need a head-wind to give them lift and so they head off into the wind, get up in the sky and then turn in the direction they actually want to go in.

Then, when they're happily up in the sky, flying towards their destination, they're off course at least 80% of the time. You see, they don't fly in a vacuum – if they did, birds would fall out of the sky for want of air! They are constantly buffeted by winds, updraughts and downdraughts and the pilot has to adjust, adjust and constantly adjust to stay on course.

We might look different from aeroplanes but we behave similarly. We often take off in the wrong direction to get where we want to go – starting in abusive families, wrong occupations, wrong relationships, wrong behaviours and/or wrong aspirations. We might not think so at the time but these "wrong" take-offs often give us the lift we need to get up into clear sky. Only then can we get to where we want to be.

With writing, so many people are immobilised by two things:

1. Can't get started
The comments are sadly consistent: "I don't know what to write

about", "What if no one likes my writing?", "How do I know what it is that I should be writing about?" and all those other complaints that hold people back from starting. Hey, it doesn't matter where you start or what you start writing. Just get started.

The aeroplane doesn't care where it's going, initially – it starts out using whatever it can to get up there and worries about direction later. So, right now, if you're stuck, I'd suggest you ride the horse in the direction it's going, use whatever wind that's blowing and just start writing. Write what comes easiest, what takes least effort and research and just get revved up and spin your wheels.

2. Being constantly off course.

Many writers (including me) worry that they don't have a particular niche, a genre that they fit into. One week they're writing a play, the next week it's poetry and the following week it's a horror novel. We're told by all sorts of well-meaning people that we should focus and get clear about what we write about. People ask us what we write about as if it's supposed to be one darned thing. Some people are built that way but most aren't. Paulo Cuelho, who has sold over 100,000,000 books, was an unsuccessful song-writer and an unsuccessful writer about black magic and he kept on writing till his truly successful writing emerged.

So, like the aeroplane that you are, keep a distant destination in mind and do not be surprised if you find yourself off course most of the time.

I don't know if you noticed, but over 90% of our aeroplanes (and Paulo Cuelho) get to where they want to be. However, they don't get there by sitting on the tarmac worrying that the wind's in the wrong direction today.

Just rev up, spin your wheels, move your pen, write some words and, on this rock I stand, the winds of fate will have you off course 80% of the time and will, eventually, bring you into land with a gentle rush and a happy pilot. Happy flying!

Contaminative Proximity & Clarity

You have a choice every moment. Choose your own truth.

I was woken in the middle of the night with a phrase zinging round in my head: contaminative proximity. I wrote it down (writers have pens and pads beside their beds for just this purpose), having no idea what it meant ... and yet, in some small, dark corner of my brain there was a certainty of knowing. I let the words rest on the paper, knowing their meaning would be made clear.

The next morning I read a story in Nury Vittachi's book, *The Shanghai Union of Industrial Mystics*:

In ancient China in the first century, a criminal was caught robbing the emperor's palace. He was sentenced to twenty days in jail. But the jail turned out to be no jail. There were only white squares painted on the ground. The robber was placed in the centre of a painted square. The only other person there was an old man with a long beard in the next square.

The robber asked, "What sort of jail is this?"

The old man said, "The worst in the world. If any convict steps outside his lines, all the demons of hell come and eat him up.

The robber was terrified. He stayed inside the painted

lines for the full twenty days. At the end of that time, the bearded man stepped out of his square.

The robber asked, "Why are you not being eaten by all the demons in hell?"

The old man said, "I am not a convict. I am a jailer."

Blade of Grass, people think they react to what is around them. But the truth is that they react to how other people react to what is around them. The worst demons live inside our minds.

You see, contaminative proximity has nothing to do with physical proximity and everything to do with how much we allow others to influence us.

And what has this to do with writing?

In a recent Linkedin forum, one writer suggested that anyone who did not use style guides was a fool. So I commented:

"*The Road* by Cormac McCarthy won the 2007 Pulitzer Prize for Fiction and the James Tait Black Memorial Prize for Fiction in 2006 ... with not a single apostrophe and a whole gamut of other style guide crimes. Cormac may find it odd you calling him a fool but who's to quibble ... they're obviously important if you decide they're important, like most things in life."

The other writer replied, "A professional writer, editor or proof-reader knows the rules, follows a given style, and is consistent – that's a service to the reader, which is what matters most to me." To her, a writer is not professional and is a fool if they don't do it a specific (her) way ... even if they're a hugely successful writer!

A few years ago, three of us found ourselves in the "party district" of our fair city, something an old man like me doesn't usually do. However, there I was with two friends in this frenetic cauldron of alcohol- and drug-enhanced hormones. Deafening music was blaring from every pub and club, groups of young people were standing around posing, shouting nonsense at each other and pretending they were blissfully and magnificently coping with their lives. Bottles and cans were bouncing into gutters, boys were playfully punching each other and girls were giggling and competing for Tart of the Night competition. Then, as we ambled amid this heaving throng, sporadic fights started and, eventually, the police arrived to be taunted by those they were trying to protect. Batons and hand-cuffs were waved about and flailing, drunk youths were carted off into the police van, their pride more damaged than their bodies.

Now, strangely, we three bemused onlookers walked right through this war of nonsense as if we were in some protective bubble. A policeman brushed my shoulder while in pursuit of a rebelling child but, apart from that, there was no contact or comments.

As we emerged from the throgging masses we looked back and wondered if it had really happened. I realised we had had a choice – join them or not. Though we had close physical proximity, our mental proximity was light years away.

We see people at funerals crying, looking sombre and acting stoically and so we feel we must behave the way they do. We don't feel like doing it but, if we allow ourselves, we can easily be sucked into something not of our making.

On England's public transport one is supposed to act as if one is the only person on the planet – no eye contact, no touching and definitely no talking. Sometimes, when I strike up a conversation, the other person is so shocked or brain-dead that no conversation ensues but, other times, I find myself in the most fascinating of conversations. Everyone else has allowed others to contaminate them and so they miss out while I and my fellow de-contaminator have a whale of a time.

Once upon a time, way back in the good old days when men were men and so were women, I was fifteen years old. It was a Maori wedding – the most fun you can have with your pants on – and it was the first time I'd played my saxophone in public, for money. We had the most exhilarating time and I crashed into bed in the wee hours at the band leader's house. At breakfast the next morning was granddad – 92-years-old with teeth missing, bad hearing, bad breath and a hit-and-miss shaving routine. Everyone was telling him to "shut up and eat you silly old bugger" and other equally dismissive comments. I think they thought they were being funny and I knew I was supposed to be treating him like that too – I was supposed to allow myself to be contaminated by their behaviour.

However, something about that old man drew me in and, again, in a bubble, I sat next to him and asked about his life. The conversation was difficult on account of his hearing and the background orchestra of derision and breakfast clatter but he told me. He had been shanghaied (stolen) from a London street at the age of fifteen and was forced to man (boy?) a square rigger. He'd sailed the world, fought in South Africa, joined gold rushes in Australia and America and, after many other adventures, had finished his working life managing a tea plantation in Ceylon. He then retired to Martinborough, New Zealand, where we all sat that fine morning.

I related his story to everyone there and the clatter and hubbub suddenly died. They were stunned and embarrassed to think they'd ignored such a fascinating man, living in their midst. They'd each allowed the others' behaviour to contaminate them and had not exercised any consciousness over the proximity of influence. If they had, they'd have been living not with a silly old bugger but an entertaining and fascinating human being.

Which all goes to show that writers and other humans can all benefit from being aware of the proximity of others' contamination and consciously creating their own behaviour. Such an entertaining and fascinating world will emerge, I suspect.

The advice here is to be in the world, not of it. Listen, absorb and then discern. Let go everything that doesn't fit into your unique keyhole. More than anything else, remain in contaminative proximity to your own soul, to your own still voice. They are never wrong.

You Might be a Writer if ...

Are you mad or just a writer?

- You can't leave home without at least two pens with you.
- You can't leave home without at least one pad with you ... two is better; a small one for your jacket or back pocket and a larger one for your bag.
- If you find yourself without a pen and pad, you're likely to scold yourself for forgetting them. Panic may set in.
- You love visiting book stores and libraries – not to buy or borrow a book but just to be with all your friends, sitting on the shelves. If someone asks why you're there, you might dutifully buy or borrow a book but that's only to prove that you're normal ... which you're not!
- You continually scan public signs for bad grammar and for illogical or ambiguous wording. When you excitedly point these out to friends they sigh and look skywards, annoyed or indulgent of your interest in such trivialities.
- You love to read books, of course, but that's only part of the larger experience – the smell, touch and look of these is a joy in itself.
- You annoy your family and friends by pausing videos to scribble down juicy phrases you hear in them ... or, if you're too scared to annoy people, you anxiously hope you can remember those juicy phrases for later.
- Words, in any language, fascinate you and you're

amazed, for example, that woman in Arabic is qahine and in Maori it's wahine – one letter different. Or that potato in Dutch and French is ground apple – aardappel in Dutch and pomme de terre in French. Others seem to find your fascination in this boring.
- You love puns and plays on words and are constantly juggling words and trying to find unusual ways of using them.
- You may not remember peoples' names but you'll remember something they said or did, working out how you can include that in a story you're writing.
- While the credits are rolling and your friends are looking for the actors' names, you're looking to see who the screen writer is.
- You like injecting new and unusual words into your conversations; not to boast but to savour their texture as you play with them.

There is something intensely sublime about chancing upon a magic moment of solitude where pad, pen and words meet, with the words congregating and filling the page with no apparent effort on your part. This can be in a busy café, crowded train or far from the maddening crowds. Whether there's others around you or not, the outer world just dissolves around you for this moment, however long it is … you might be a writer!

Writing is not Homeopathy

The sport of finding your own voice

Writing is not homeopathy – less is not better.
Writing is a sport – more is better.

You don't see Usaine Bolt sitting by the track, watching other runners, hoping to absorb their fitness. No, he is one of those runners, slogging round the track, day after day. He runs and he runs and he runs. And he gets better at running.

Writing's a sport and the best way to improve is to stand by and watch others, hoping to absorb their greatness ... No. It. Is. Not! To write well you've gotta' write and write and write.

It often starts out as drivel, childish drivel, but keep on drivelling and it will become something else. It will become you.

Most of us have learned the rules of writing from others: Don't start sentences with and. And don't start sentences with but. But you must only have one and in a list. Don't use archaic words like thou and henceforth and thee. And, henceforth, all sentences will have a verb and a noun. Avoid abbreviations. Lotsa' rules.

That's fine as it gave you some basics to pin your hat on.

However, our heads grow and childhood hats no longer fit. Rules are there for a purpose – to get you up and running till you can, with experience, form your own. You see, lights at a pedestrian crossing are good for children who have little perception of vehicle speeds and spatial proximity. For adults, those lights are for the stupid who can't make their own decisions.

The same for writing rules. You start with them to give you direction when you have none. Then, as you cross the road for the hundredth time – or write your 100,000th word – you realise you can leave people and rules behind and skip gaily across a carless road while the pedants wait for a light bulb to control their lives.

You can't, however, move comfortably into your own rules until you've crossed you own road enough times to forget the rules.

You see, when you turn up at the page, put pen to paper over and over and over again, something happens. Whether you choose 500 words a day, 2,000 words a day or 5,000 words a day, the discipline of doing it, doing it, doing it, will guarantee something arises in you – something beyond old, other-people rules. As you gain confidence in your wordiness (worthiness?) and lose that childish self-consciousness, this indefinable beingness will move through your pen and into your words and phrases.

You'll find your own pace, your own unique phrasings and style. You'll invent new words. Your sentences will start with banned words and they'll be beautiful. Or taut with anger. Or gripping. Or flowingly loquacious and gently sweet ... whatever you want them to be.

As you practise your sport – as you let loose the words you have inside you, all around you – you'll find they take over, they do the work. It doesn't become effortless for it's always damned hard work. But, through the effort of leaving the enticing world for a time each day – to lay down sodding word after sodding word – you'll find the traffic lights are red and there are no cars; you can skip across a rule, take a shorter way, a longer way, a different way.

The way will come to you and that way is what we call your voice – your particular, peculiar and enchanting way of arranging the words.

However, that way does not come to the pedant, obediently waiting for the green light. It comes to those who cross on red lights, having narrow misses, playing with possibilities and letting go as the 100,000th word stretches itself out on the paper and sighs with gratitude to you.

The first word won't do that. The 1,000th word won't do that. The 10,000th word won't do that. But the 100,000th just might.

Yes, go to your writing classes. Read the books on writing. Learn the rules. Talk to writers. Go and do all the vicarious stuff for it certainly helps.

But what really helps and what there is no substitute for is writing, writing, writing.

There. Is. No. Alternative. Write. Write. Write.

Beware The Writing Police

I don't know the writing rules so I'm not a good writer

I had to laugh. It was Sunday and, on our way into Oxford, were signs saying that there could be congestion next Friday as there was going to be a demonstration. How did they know? Council permits!

I thought protests and demonstrations were against authority! But these English protesters went cap in hand, meekly and compliantly, to pay the exorbitant fee and ask the authority if they could protest against said authority! The English have gone to war against police states, fascist regimes and dictatorships, little realising their wee country has become one.

And what has that to do with writing? Simply that Wordland has become a fascist state and, like England, it's crept up on us so subtly, so cleverly, we haven't noticed. And, like the English, it's stifling creativity. I hear so many budding writers put off writing because of the rules thrown at them.

I've been told off for using dots ... you know, when someone can't think of what to say next. I use them to slow the text down to the speed of the story to help the reader to ... aah ... to connect with the mind of the speaker.

I've been reprimanded for use of hyphens – there's a rule about them, apparently – as I've used too many per page. Nobody's quite sure why the rule exists – there's just a rule so obey it!

And single-word sentences are forbidden. Seriously. Single. Word. Sentences! I use them to stop the flow, momentarily. Or when someone's angrily stamping their feet and saying, "Stop. That. This. Instant!"

And starting sentences with and. That's naughty too.

But but is worse to start sentences with!

However, Cormac McCarthy used no speech marks (inverted commas) in The Road and millions of readers have enjoyed his book. I found it mildly confusing but, thankfully, there were only two speakers. Other books I have started and gave up on had more speakers, no inverted commas and it was just too hard keeping up with what was narrative, which was conversation and who was conversing with whom.

However, that's just my preference and if others like it, all power to creativity. I'm certainly not going to promulgate a rule about it ... or about anything else. I've got a life.

So, timid writer, please, please, please don't ever stop (or not start) because you don't know all the rules of writing, for two reasons:

Firstly, there are no rules. There are what are called conventions which are not rules but things that people have worked out, over time, that work better than other things – like writing left to right, breaking text up into readable chunks called paragraphs and full-stops and capital letters to help, again, with that chunking thing. However, if you want to write your 80,000-word novel as one long sentence and readers love it, go for it. Stick your finger up at the authorities, make your protest and be creative – we might all learn something

Secondly ... I can't climb into the minds of writers but I strongly suspect this ... it's an excuse to stop writing. There are many fears that keep us from writing – fear of success, of failure, of judgement, of giving up our accustomed discomfort – and it can feel easier to pretend it's about someone's rules and not about our own fears.

If you're a member of the Save The Apostrophe Society or the Ban The Hyphen Collective, your "good" intentions are not good at all. You're a part of a fascist society and we need more creativity, not less.

And if you're a writer, don't let the rules stop you. They didn't stop Cormac McCarthy and thousands of other writers who thumbed their noses at convention and succeeded.

Just get writing – conventional or radical – and know that whether you do or you don't, the fear will still be there. What will go away when you start, however, is the bitterness for not starting, for not stepping out, not standing for who you are. If you don't stand for something, you'll fall for anything, like the compliant Oxford protesters.

STORYTELLING RULES

My English isn't good and I don't know the rules of writing

Once upon a time a storyteller momentarily forgot how to start a story and so he wrote:

In the year of the Great Flood, a family of geese took to the air, not quite knowing where they were going …

His master, a great storytelling teacher, saw this and was aghast. "What on earth are you doing?" he asked. "You know that all stories must start with 'Once upon a time', and here you are writing something entirely different. It just cannot be done!"

"I'm very sorry", said the storyteller, "but I forgot how to start and then my quill just started moving, so I followed it. The story just seemed to be writing itself."

"If we let that happen, young man, we'll end up with all sorts of silly stories about ideas we've never heard of and with endings that aren't 'happily ever after'," said the master, going very red.

Very embarrassed, the storyteller tried to write the correct words but his pen had its own story:

Strangely unconcerned at their lack of direction they simply flew – no one leading and no one following and all in unison, a rhythm of flight. As they rose together, they felt a beautiful sense of friendship. As their wings caressed the air they soared with effortless grace and an eagle looked down and wondered.

This Master of the Skies looked down and sighed in admiration as he watched these beautiful geese stretch their minds and bodies in joy. He knew they had nowhere to go but, somehow, he also knew, in an instant of knowing, that there was somewhere special they were headed, something magic he just couldn't put a claw on ...

"You have not listened, have you!" croaked the old Master of Stories. "You change the opening lines and now your characters are going nowhere. The readers must know what's happening and why, and you must have a definite end in view. Readers need certainty. Create it!"

"I'm ... I'm sorry sir, I just can't seem to control this story," pleaded the storyteller. "It just seems to have a mind of its own."

"Well, get your own mind and direct your story," commanded the Master. "This school has a reputation of scholarly control and storytelling tradition to uphold."

"I'll really try ..." said the storyteller.

But as the geese flew on, his pen sped on and he knew it wasn't his story. He was simply being used for something more beautiful than he could imagine.

As the eagle looked down on these soaring geese, he had an irrepressible urge to share in their joy of flight. But, in his mind, he knew that geese and eagles didn't fly together and the turmoil in his mind disturbed him as he battled between his new and beautiful urge and his strong ancient rules.

At the same time, the geese, without looking up, could sense the Master of the Skies admiring them and their hearts expanded as they imagined the one they had always admired, joining them in flight. As their thoughts went skywards, the eagle's great shadow flowed over the four soaring geese, somehow uniting them in a togetherness they had never known before. With craggy brown above and smooth grey below, this new creature of five creatures banked and turned in a graceful oneness. They dived a little and rose again and, in their silence, their communication was complete. In each dive, soar, turning, stalling and accelerating there was perfect coordination and togetherness. The five flew as one.

As the Master of Stories came back into the room, the young man hid his paper and pretended to be starting again on a blank paper. A vaguely approving "Humph!" came from the Master as he walked on. The young man's pen took off again ...

As the eagle, sighting a mouse, broke away, dived, pounced and rose again to the flying four. It took a little time and some effort to catch up with them as they were speeding as no goose had ever done before. The Master of the Skies was confused and exalted by this new experience, which seemed to have a strange magnetic pull for all of them – to where, none of them knew.

As the shadows began to lengthen below, the soaring five heeled over and started gently spiraling down. In the joy of their flight, they hadn't realized how high they had gone – higher than the eagle had ever gone before. It seemed to take forever to alight on the waiting land – a place they had never been before but a place that had an eerily familiar feel about it.

The eagle had captured several rodents during the day and was full, but the geese were hungry and munched ravenously on the succulent green grass. As the smiling sun ascended in golden, then orange farewell, they all became aware of two quiet people sitting by the lakeside, some distance away. One was an old man with a long gray beard and the other was a younger, fresh-faced man, and the stillness and peace the sky people felt from these two-leggeds drew them closer. They'd never been near human creatures before and their first instinct was to move away but, strangely, they also felt strongly drawn to these unmoving and unspeaking men. Still greedily munching on the delicious grass, the geese soon found themselves beside the men, as the eagle landed on a log beside them all.

"We're glad you've arrived. We've been waiting for you all for some days." said the old man, still looking across the lake as it turned from orange to black in the last rays of the sun.

The young man smiled, knowing the truth of these words and wondering how he knew these things. For two days he had known to expect visitors but had not imagined they'd be birds.

"It's wonderful to see you, my friends," said the old man, "but you must feed your hunger and quench your thirst before we talk. We have plentiful time and there's no need to hurry."

The geese felt contentment in these words and quietly went back to nibbling on the familiar grass and some strange but tasty plants. The eagle simply perched on the log, filling his soul with the nourishing peace and friendship that flowed around and through him. There was no need for words as the three sat and looked upon the water, glistening in the rising moon.

"So where's this silly story going now?" demanded the Master of Stories.

The storyteller almost fell off his stool in shock, not realising that his teacher had been watching over his shoulder.

"Oh, aah, um ... I don't really know. I ... I'm trying to make it controlled and predictable like you said but my pen just keeps going elsewhere," stammered the storyteller.

"Humph," said the teacher, with a little softness in his voice.

The storyteller, slightly relieved, awaited his pen's movement but nothing happened. Stillness. Nothing. With a frown, he looked around and, as his eyes followed a rafter, he felt an imperceptible movement, a twinge and gently, his nib formed a word, then another and, slowly, a whole sentence was etched on to the paper.

The pen told of the eagle's mixture of emotions.

These two-leggeds had been feared for they had always killed the sky people and taken their eggs but here he was, sitting next to the most peaceful and loving beings he had ever known. Somehow, the love was stronger than the fear and he found his closed eyes filling with tears – a strange and cleansing sensation. The young man held out his hand and the eagle rubbed the side of his face against the upturned palm.

The geese finished eating and came to rest in front of the

men and the eagle, on the sand, and all seven looked across the lake. As the moon rose before them and shone her beams across the lake to them, they absorbed the gentle light and a humming began. This strange yet familiar sound gently permeated their souls, cells and senses. It enlivened and calmed, rejuvenated and restored, calmed and settled. It came from nowhere and everywhere.

The young man, waiting for his master to speak, discovered insistent words, seeking release. In embarrassment, he tried to hold them back, but they pushed forward, wanting to be heard. In the time with this beautiful old man, he had felt great magic, new sproutings of awareness and a hearing and seeing of things not sensed before. These persistent words were yet another unravelling of the mystery and as he gave into their request, he awaited the result with interest and unease. He let his mouth open and a resonant new voice stepped forth from him:

"There are many sounds in your world, my friends, and you may be irritated by discordant arguing, painful cries and sorrowing sobs. Or, you may be elevated by happy laughter, beautiful music and contented sighs. But these, my friends, are the outward sounds of your world. Still yourself, listen to them, listen into them and hear the sounds behind the sounds. As you quieten your mind, you'll discover a world you can't detect with your senses but it's there, more solidly than any other. Listen to it, sense it, savour it. Then let it sing through you and your words."

The Master of Stories, quietly behind the storyteller, smiled at a story the broke the rules ... a story where nothing happened ... and he seemed to have damp cheeks. He nodded and the young storyteller smiled.

COMMUNICATING TO CONFUSE

I'm not sure if I can explain things clearly

For the Authors, Writers, Publishers, Editors, & Writing Professionals group on LinkedIn, the rules state: "There are only four rules. No spamming, no flaming and no discussion regarding politics, social issues, and/or religion". I asked what flaming meant and, after much discussion, found that it has a multitude of meanings, including the one meant here – being offensive. Bringing all the different meanings of flaming together, it actually means an extremely drunk, flamboyant, gay male who is insulting and confrontational.

I asked why they didn't use the word offensiveness and the writers of these rules blamed the internet and the growth of a whole new vocabulary, intimating that they had no choice but to go along with using the same obscure words that others do. No! They have a choice and, as writers, it needs to be toward better communication, not worse.

This is our world and we can choose to lead, not follow ... sorry, I'm preaching and that's not what this book is about. What it is about is finding your soul and its purest expression. That doesn't come from following ... well, from following anyone but our true selves ... bother, there I go preaching again!

The point of communication, I thought, was to make things clearer, not more ambivalent. As writers, it behoves us not to take a back seat, using what the lowest common denominators use, but to take the steering wheel and practice what we preach by actually communicating – simply and clearly.

Then I picked up a booklet advertising the exhibits at the North Wall Arts Centre, Oxford, UK, for spring 2012. One of the artists was described: "Ruth's artistic practice investigates the convergence between contemporary art and the sciences ... explores ideas of complexity, abundance and man's perception of the nature ... she explores how apparent randomness belies the organic patterns contained within the intricacy of life and traces the harmonics hidden in the detail, as she examines the simultaneous simplicity and complexity of the universe."

Lots of exploring and tracing but little sense.

Now, the writer and/or the artist are either laughing their heads off at the gullibility and stupidity of art connoisseurs – or those pretending to be – or they have no idea what they're talking about. No matter how many times you read that, no sense will arise.

There will always be those who choose to obscure what they're saying – if, indeed, they're saying anything at all – but none of us needs to follow them. Aargghh, there I go again – preaching! I'll stop right now!

Try, in all ways, to follow the KISS method – Keep It Simple, Sweetheart!

Turn Up At The Page

I don't have time to write a novel

People tell me that they'd love to write a book, that they've always dreamed of writing, that others say they should write a book ... and so I say, "Do it!"

And the standard reply?

"Oh, yes, I'd love to but I just don't have the time right now – writing a book takes a lot of time."

Yes, writing a book does take a lot of time but so does watching your favourite TV soap! However, like watching that important soap, you don't have to do it all the time. You just do a little every day. If you really want to write something – a poem, an article, a book – you have to drop the self-defeating excuses, turn up at the page and start writing.

My second book, *Whose Life Is It Anyway?*, was written over breakfast, every morning, for a year. A half hour's writing of 500-1,000 words, every day, produced enough words for two novels – in one year.

Everyone's busy and we all have the perfect excuses for not doing what we'd really love to do. Why? Because having a project completed then sets us up for fear of failure and/or fear of success. Most people would rather avoid those fears by retreating behind a myriad of invalid excuses. Wouldn't you rather end your life with memories rather than dreams?

So, think about all the little spaces in your life – over

breakfast, while commuting, in cafés, watching TV – which you can turn into sacred writing spaces. Oh, but you'll then come up with that other Grand Excuse – "I want to write but I don't know what to write about ." You will never know what to write about till you start writing. Don't wait for the writing – it's waiting for you.

If you have a desire to write, you know exactly what to write about – the what will reveal itself when you turn up at the blank page (or blank computer screen) and start writing. If you don't know what to write, write exactly that ...

"I don't know what to write but I've started writing and, though I have no clue why I'm here doing this I have, at least, turned up at the page and my pen's moving (keyboard's clacking) and making word-marks on the blank paper/screen and nothing's coming to me yet but I'm going to keep writing because Philip said if I did, the what, the subject would come to me ..."

Just keep your pen moving, your keyboard busy, and, at the start, it could be complete drivel, utter senseless rubbish. You might write about the horrible/beautiful weather, your uncomfortable writing chair, your slow computer, your cranky father, your last holiday, your biggest dream, your worst moment ... it doesn't matter what you write but keep doing it and – on this rock I stand – the ideas will come. You see, there is a theory that thoughts create words. It's wrong – words create thoughts which create words which create thoughts which create words which create thoughts which create words ...

So, throw out your excuses, substitute waste spaces for write spaces and turn up at the page. You'll be amazed at what you unleash when you turn up and write something, then something else, then something else ...

Writing On Empty

I always get writer's block. I keep getting stuck.

When there's nothing to write, when I'm empty, I still write. There may not be a subject, a story or a concern. There's just the soft and exquisite pleasure of watching my pen flow across the page, an army of blue squiggles marching after it in double-quick time. The army grows quickly: first, a soldier, one word, then soon a platoon a company and a brigade and, as I flip the page, I have the Emperor's army marching in silent obedience to my pen's leadership. I do nothing. I observe the growing battalions and volunteer my arm, my hand, for the pen's march over page after page.

This army or words is, however, no ordinary army. It is not for attack. It does not defend. In fact, army may be quite the wrong word for it as no guns are carried, no orders shouted, no ranks defined. The words simply lie there, rippling on the page, defenceless and willing ... willing to serve any who would read, absorb, enjoy.

451 degrees Fahrenheit would see these words obliterated in flame as would my spilt coffee or your scorning, turned-away look. They may last a split second or a longer eon – they have no care. They will serve or not serve, amuse or not amuse, inform or not inform. To some it's gibberish, to some profound. To some kinda' weird, to some sorta' fascinating. To some pointless, to some meaningful. To some jarring, to some soothing.

The words don't care and I try not to but kinda' do and sorta' hope you do, knowing you mightn't.

Of the uncountable squillions and heptazillions of words expressed in this wee corner of the universe, they really don't rate. And yet they do.

For example, today, I was empty but on a mission. I needed a battalion but couldn't rouse one soldier from his bed.

They said write a story about JEALOUSY in under 500 words. My brain stumbled over itself, thought only of Humpty Dumpty and I gave up. Don't ask me why it thought about Humpty Dumpty - it just did!

When there's a blockage in the plumbing, forcing more rubbish down the pipe never helps! I needed, as usual, to let the emptiness vacuum it clean.

This is not a technique that has come easily for I've always felt the need to take action, to do stuff, to undo stuff. I've never considered not-doing stuff or doing not-stuff. It just never occurred to me.

A Course in Miracles undid that for me when, among other things, it talked of the two choices we have:
1. Doing it (anything) in our own power, or
2. Giving over to that which is bigger than us, whatever we want to call it.

I'd always done things in my own power and look where that got me … powerless and stuck in the plumbing of life … and keeping that greater power impotent and at bay.

The kak in the pipes does not flush itself out; it needs something beyond its own filth. When I'm the blockage, more of me doesn't help! So I attempt to stop thinking.

Less of me – or less of my thinking – gives permission for the Big Plumber to thrust their brush down my pipes and allow the resulting vacuum to draw in fecundity of spirit and creativity of mind.

I empty myself but not by not thinking. Our minds, busy little sods that they are, cannot not think. Asking a mind to not think is like asking a fish not to swim. Thinking is what minds must do if they're to continue existing.

We cannot empty our minds by not-thinking thoughts, by thinking not-thoughts or by not thinking. We can only continue by entertaining other-thinking-thoughts and the blockage – writers block – is sucked clean and shining new.

So, back to this soldierless day - I changed my thoughts away from what I'm "supposed" to be writing, away from JEALOUSY, away from writing and anything else related. But Humpty Dumpty stayed there, lodged in the U-bend of my pipes while the rest of the gunk dissolved and washed away. Humpty Dumpty was unmoved by my mind rushing off to think of holiday plans, disgust at management behaviour at work or the tragedy of the Australian fires. After two days of not-writing-thinking, Mr Dumpty was still staring in at me through my windscreen, whatever way my mind steered and swerved.

So I gave in, started writing the old Humpty Dumpty rhyme, aware that it had nothing to do with JEALOUSY and I didn't care. I just kept writing.

Well, by the end of the second line, I noticed my pen deviating, clunking onto another track. The third line was a small deviation and, from there, the old rhyme was left far behind. This is what came out:

> Humpty Dumpty sat on a wall
> Humpty Dumpty had a great fall
> Crash bang that's all
> Oops, not the end a'tall
> T'was the Mexican wall of Senor Trump
> From which Humpty boy went thump
> See, Mr Humpty's a drug boss, CSI moaned
> Investigators left no turn unstoned
> Was no accident, t'was Donald's pusher
> They kept the secret, quieter than husher
> Humpy was suspected of lotsa', lotsa' stuff

Got Trumpy in a wild old huff
Like who Melania was amorously courted
Humpy had her naked, got her sorted
Civilian planes, no one knew who shootin'
Was no other than Vladimir Putin
But Trumpy, see, he got the blame
For starting World War III, he wanted no fame
But others smarter than the president chookie
Were setting him up, playing him hookie
And jealousy's a cruel, twisted master
His anger got his heart beating faster
Someone must pay for back-stabbing games
Save humiliation, stop feeling the shames
Thrashing about, any target will do
When you're fuming, stuck in a stew
Donald had suspicions, who's loving his wife
So they're firing-line first, pay with their life
Then Humpty's up at the wall, carrying Mexican drugs
Sticks his head up, easy shot for Donald's thugs
So now he's scrambled, cracked and broke
But Donald chose the wrong, wrong bloke
Of the many, many innocent folk
Wasn't the one hiding a yolk
But the egg smell turned Trump's mind to mess
Was, in fact, Australian egg boy, no less
So, when your dander's up and jealousy's ripe
Check your facts, not your nose … and not the hype!

See, it's absolute drivel. Total nonsense. But I now felt strangely happy and free. Having silly fun with drivel, my pipes emptied and were clean and ready for me to continue my Great Australian Novel, *Scars Don't Sweat*.

So, if you need to take a silly, inconsequential diversion, for a moment, do it. You'll then find you can return to your "serious" story much easier. Just an idea …

CREATE SPACES

I never get in the mood for writing, though I want to

People wonder how the events, characters, ideas and dramas come to writers so they can write them down. I don't know the answer to this question but, for me, there are some quite specific things I can do to allow them to enter my space, for capture on a blank page of paper. The first is turning up at the page and the second is Creating Spaces, covered here:

I loved writing at school and then stopped doing it. Actually, I stopped doing it and also forgot that I'd enjoyed it. I always wrote long, interesting letters home to my parents and enjoyed the process of that. I didn't, however, link that enjoyment to any desire or ability to be a published author. I just loved writing and kept doing it.

Then, many years later, I started meditation. The discipline of doing that each morning and evening started an internal discipline – I started listening and being aware of the thoughts, feelings and moments of greatness that passed through my mind.

The daily act of meditation also imbued me with an openness of mind. It dawned slowly and sometimes it didn't dawn at all! However, there came into my mind, each time I sat in stillness and silence, a reverence and a remembrance of my greater self which floated in and rested there with its graceful presence. Even when it felt tiny, fleeting and distant, its creative beingness moved me.

Then, somewhere in the space of presence, a recalling (a calling?) started to speak through the clamour of constant chatter. This still, quiet voice of my recall began to speak louder and louder. It felt, at times, as if the large, gentle hand of God was at my back, urging me forward to something. I knew not what this something might be – or was I just afraid of acknowledging I had something to accomplish? – but I knew a presence more potent and knowing than I was urging me on.

As I allowed the daily rush of rabid rubbish to fall from my mind, the void allowed my silent calling to float to the surface. Eventually, that calling voice inspired action.

After a week or so, a sentence popped into my mind and refused to leave. It doggedly nagged at my mind till I wrote it down. It kept happening. At times I would leave it for days, challenging it to stay with me – it always did. I hated rising in the early morning – probably because of the freezing mornings I'd had to rise to go mustering or on lambing beats, in my childhood – but that's when the sentences would climb into my brain and play their constant, cheerful and annoying tune.

Eventually I would succumb. I would get up at five am, sit at my desk and write down the stupid sentence. As I was writing that one, another sentence would arrive and so I'd write that too ... an hour later I'd pull away from that beautiful reverie, mind and pen in holy relationship, and see the pile of previously blank paper, now happily replete with words.

Having little idea of what I'd written, I'd make a space in my day and type my scribbles into the computer. Sometimes, when typing, I'd decide to "improve" the wording. Then, as I read the typed words back, I'd realise the original ones were better – always, the originals were better.

You see, we all have busy lives, things to do, things to plan, things to worry about. We've all got incomes to make, families to feed, relationships to nurture, skills to learn, holidays to endure, toys to buy ... and on and on the list goes. Our minds are kept conveniently busy with the doings of or little world.

These doings help us avoid the bigger world we wish to inhabit. It takes courage to let that rush of rabid rubbish go for a while – even for milliseconds – in order to peer into the void of our greatest possibilities.

Many writers choose solitude – a cottage on a remote coastline, for example – to listen to their muses. There are more subtle and less treacherous ways of letting the clamouring crowd of cackles go, of achieving solitude of mind. Meditation works for me and, with years of practice, I can easily write in a noisy cafe or commuter train. I'm aware of the outer noise but my inner dialogue is never stilled by it, now.

Whether your gift to the world is in politics, art, sport, business or in any other area of life, I'd suggest you find some way, any way, to rise through the daily din to that deep desire of a life lived creatively. Whether it's meditation, seclusion, music, an absorbing hobby or whatever, find a way to drop the dross and raise the recall – you'll be amazed at what's waiting for you from your greater self.

Writers Block and the Kaleidoscope Life

What if I can't make myself write or I can't think of anything?

The laser-like focus on my writing has always bothered me ... mainly because I don't have it.

I feel jealous of people who are born knowing what they want to do in life, get on and do it all their life and do it happily and successfully.

A colleague was telling me about a Jewish fabric importer in Sydney who, at 92, still goes to work by hopping in his wheelchair and wheeling himself in, accompanied by his beloved and trusty dog. A big part of me is envious of people who find their mission and just keep doing it like Sir Laurence Olivier who died, of old age, on stage, doing what he loved.

The way I've been built, it seems, is that I find my focus, lose it, find another focus, lose that, find another, lose that and return to the first one for a while. It has meant, of course, that my life has been a series of adventures – some related, some unrelated to others – which include, among other things, being an accountant in New Zealand, a horse and camel trekker in Australia, a corporate trainer in England, a publisher in New Zealand, an AIDS workshop co-facilitator in South Africa, a lecturer in England and a teacher in Australia.

It has made for a fascinatingly varied and interesting life. It might seem that I'm a bit unbalanced but, in fact, I'm totally balanced – I've had exactly the same number of divorces as marriages (three each way!) so there's been a lot of fascination and variety going on there too.

I honour the life I've had ... or fragments of many lives, perhaps ... and I don't regret a moment of it.

My dissatisfaction comes in when I try to measure my success (e.g. income, numbers of books sold, numbers of books written, offers from publishers or writers agents, followers to this blog or my Facebook page and so on) and then weigh that up against reality, like an accountant comparing budgeted income against actual income. Every time I fall short of myself ... fall short of myself? Now, isn't that a stupid phrase! I am what I am and so there's no distance between me and me; not even a shadow from a distant sun. I've done what I've done, I've thought what I've thought, I've said what I've said, I am what I am. $I = I$ and I cannot fall short (or long) of myself. That's the logic and it's irrefutable.

What's also irrefutable is the feeling that I haven't done as well as I think I should have and maybe, just maybe, I should stop thinking, stop expecting, stop judging and then my irrefutable feelings will slip into line with my irrefutable logic.

It's my thinking, expecting and judging that calculates my apparent lack of success as being equated with my diffuse-like (is that the opposite of laser-like?) focus and, if I'd decided on one thing and done one thing, I'd be a screaming success and not a screaming meme.

That was my noisy dissatisfaction speaking – always first and always louder than my Deeper Wisdom.

And then that still, quiet voice that always speaks second, always waits for the loud voice of judgement to wear itself thin, whispers its disarming truth I cannot refute – if I'd not had a life of variety, I would not have the wide experience from which to draw my stories from. If I'd been a fabric importer or an accountant all my life, I'd have had so much less to write about and may have run out of stories after one book.

Writers, you see, are strange creatures. We can write about things (from the outside) or we can write within things (from the inside). The perspective inside my experience is infinitely more juicy, verdant and fecund than the view from outside. The difference between stories about (which academics write) and stories within (which wordsmiths write) are that our juices are stirred more by those who are in there looking out than those who are out there looking in.

As I consider where the juice comes from for my stories, my judgement, expectations and logic cannot refute that a kaleidoscope life, a life of turmoil, could not but bring juice to a book or, in my case, several books.

A straight and singular life may make one successful in fabric importing and accounting but it's not necessarily so for the creative, plucking-stories-out-of-thin-air career of a writer.

Writers of more straight-line lives – Jane Austen, John Grisham and Stephen King, for example – have become extremely successful but the kaleidoscope one I've chosen to inhabit, by default, has certainly given me plenty of gristle to chew on and write about.

The next question, then, is, "Why don't I just shut up and get on with writing these irrefutably fascinating stories rather than warbling on about them?" The simple answer is that I had writers block and, when I have that, I stop writing stories, relax, get a coffee, look at what's bothering me most and write that down. That takes the worry from my head and out onto the paper, leaving a large mind-space to draw the stories into. In fact, as I pen these words, I feel another story coming on.

And so have you … pick one event in your life, embroider it and write as if you're writing about yourself in the third person. Change your name, if you like, and change the names of other characters and places, if you like. For just one moment, become an omnipresent God, looking down on you with a benign smile.

If it was an amusing event, make it hilarious, stupid and add in complications and stumbling fools to make it slap-stick. If it was a sad or angry event, make it more so with crazy, unreasonable people and situations crowded in.

Whatever the event, tart it up to make it more vivid, more memorable, more ... well, more different that the reality.

It's a cathartic and freeing experience and, by the end, you may have a darned good yarn to share around.

Enjoy!

The Bitch On Your Shoulder

I'm too critical of myself to take the risk

Have you got a bitch on your shoulder? Most people have. It's that constantly nagging voice that tells you you're doing it all wrong, you're not good enough, you won't make it, you shouldn't try, that everyone else is more deserving, clever, beautiful and important than you. You recognise it now? Of course you do – you may not call it your bitch but you recognise it by the tireless drivel it fills your mind with ... mindless and demeaning filth about your total unworthiness and inability to function as a mature adult.

The sad thing is that most people listen to and act on the lies this serpent hisses into their ears. Only a few people choose to wake up to the fact that it's lies, damned lies, and these tend to be people who persist and succeed where others give up.

Several years ago I did the Landmark personal development course and one of the many exercises was to identify the main conversation we have with ourselves. Of course, our bitch tells us many things but each person has a favourite phrase:

I'm too fat
I'm ugly
I'll never be a success
I can't remember things
I'm too short
I'm not bright enough

My phrase, once I'd uncovered it, was, "Who am I that anybody would want to listen to me?" And here I was, trying to be a writer, "knowing" that nobody would listen to me! How self-sabotaging could that be!

So, once we had found our favourite conversation – our favourite, negative self-talk – we went around the room introducing ourselves to the 30 other people there by shaking hands, saying our name and then our favourite conversation. Once you've met 30 people and introduced yourself 30 times with ...

Hello, I'm Shirley and I'm too fat. Hello, I'm Shirley and I'm too fat. Hello, I'm Shirley and I'm too fat ... or

Hello, I'm Michael and I'm not bright enough. Hello, I'm Michael and I'm not bright enough. Hello, I'm Michael and I'm not bright enough ...

You might imagine the mirth in the room – it was rocking with our laughter. You see, once you get that silent, snarling conversation out of your head, through your mouth and over to someone else, you realise just how stupid it is. In fact, try it right now – say your favourite, demeaning self-talk out loud, to yourself in the mirror. As you say it, you'll smile and wonder how or why you ever listened to it before. Say it again and again and your smile will soon turn to a belly laugh as the insanity of the whole thing is revealed.

And then we are surprised that writers agents, publishers and the reading public don't accept us! Maybe they're not making their own choices. Maybe, just maybe, they're simply reflecting the rejection we're sending to ourselves, every waking second of our lives. One way to find out is to:
1. Acknowledge the stories we're filling our heads with,
2. See them for what they are (just stories) and laugh at the small, mad idea of them, and
3. Find a grander, more real story to tell ourselves ... and see how our world changes.

After all, what do we have to lose apart from regret at a life not lived ... a dream not followed?

A Gardener Tidies His Garden

Keeping myself going by making my progress public

Once upon a time there was a boy who lived beside the winding Awhea river, in the shadow of the Wakapuni hill ... and many other hills, in the bottom of New Zealand's North Island. This was a land of hills, green in winter and brown in summer. So many hills that the 22,000-acre farm this boy was born on was called Lagoon Hills. In that vast acreage only one paddock, two acres, was flat. The rest of the land went up or down, depending on what direction you rode your horse.

This boy had a hero from a flat and distant land, from a flat and distant time. This hero had been given many guises and meanings and the one this boy had was of a man in sandals and a long white robe, walking the dusty miles, giving hope, peace and healing at all who asked. Like any hero, worshippers had built shrines and religions to him and, though his message was of peace and forgiveness, these religions fought with each other and judged each other as sinful. For this reason, mainly, the boy stayed away from these religions and shrines and he stayed with the man - the good man with nothing bad to say against anyone, the man who called all to help all, the man whose greatest strength was his defencelessness ... the greatest strength there is.

That boy is now a man - older but not necessarily wiser - near the winding Windrush river, in the shadow of no hills, for the Windrush meanders through a land flat and green and laden with trees. This man is a gardener; a gardener of words which grow in his fertile mind. Great words, silly words, helpful words, serious words, funny words ... they all grow there in profusion both beautiful and untidy.

The time has come, thinks the man, to start weeding, to set the plants in line, in patterns, so they can be more easily enjoyed by himself and others. So many words, so many stories, but the man is determined to set his garden in order ... his many gardens in order. Some gardens are small ones, short stories, to be enjoyed on a quick walk. Some gardens are larger, novels, to linger over with smiles, sadness, laughter and insight. Each garden is different and so this gardener must decide which to tend to first, which to prune and hoe and water first.

This man is a good gardener – some say a great gardener of words. However, he's a brilliant starter and not prone to finishing projects. A book, a garden or any other project takes time and, at times, seems never-ending. It's easy for a starter-of-projects to not finish them and it's difficult to live with a dozen unfinished projects. My soul yearns for a finished project.

That's what I wrote in 2011 when I was living in Oxfordshire, UK. I continued writing ...

If I commit to publish 1,000 words a day, with all of you looking over my shoulder, I will have to finish at least one garden for you all to enjoy. My soul will then sigh with the contentment and peace my hero engenders.

So, I have started with the garden of Arthur Bayly, a good man in satisfactory but boring job and a satisfactory but boring marriage; a man to whom the exciting events he dreams of - James Bond-type events - are about to happen. Here is the garden, the story, of Arthur Bayly as I (the man), the gardener, weed, prune, dig, replant and bring out the best of Arthur Bayly's garden for you to enjoy as you wish ... the first 1,000 words today ...

I put up the 1,000 words I wrote each morning, in the blog.

The idea was that, with the eyes of the world on me, following my progress, I became more accountable and focussed. It worked as I finished the novel, The Last Stand Down, and had it published within the year. That novel has since rewritten as a stage play. We're making a podcast of it and hope – a big, hairy hope – to have it turned into a movie.

Just another idea for you ...

I Am Such a Perfectionist

I'll never let my book be finished

Firstly, don't use the word perfectionist. Use the word frightened. Okay? So, say it again:

"I am so frightened, I'll never let my book be finished.

You see, the world is untidy, life is untidy, relationships are untidy. That's how it is. Everything is untidy, unexpected and never quite right. We're all walking with time-bombs in our pockets, never certain when they'll go off.

Any day, any minute, we can be told we're redundant, our marriage is over, we have a health scare or that something's happened to someone close to us.

The world is illogical, unfair and messy as hell. There's child slavery, sexual abuse, political corruption, environmental savagery and a limitless list of other insanities parading themselves before us. The world has always been insane and it always will be.

We try (we really do try) to control one part of our little world – our spouses, children, dogs, cats, job, health, emotions – and we can't even manage that! They're all so untidy!

The same with your story, with your book. It is habitually out of control. You sit down to write a particular scene and it takes off in an unexpected direction. You create a "nice" character and, without your permission, he does a despicable thing ... despite the fact that it's your hand controlling the pen or the keyboard!

The only healthy thing to do is to is to accept what is – accept that your planned story will not write itself in the way you want it to …

"What?" you exclaim in anguish. "My story write itself? That's blasphemy! I write the story, not the other way around!"

"No you don't!" I exclaim back. "Your story called you and you – not anyone else – volunteered for it. You volunteered to have your life experiences (all the ups and downs), the qualifications, relationships, aspirations and broken dreams that brought you to this blank page, to this story. It is only you – this unique you – who can pen this epistle to yourself and others. Even if it's not about you, even if it's a fiction, the story has you weaved through it somehow. No one else can write it for it needs the untidy randomness and variety your beautiful life has brought you."

Your hand on the pen or keyboard is the road this story must travel on. Your fascinating, quirky life is the motor to drive the story and your motivation is the fuel for that motor. However, you do not hold the steering wheel. The story does. The story needs the road, the motor and the fuel but it holds the map. It holds the steering wheel.

This is an untidy concept for we so much want to control the story. It is the least we can control in this bizarrely dysfunctional world.

Weirdly, we try to set ourselves up against the might of the universe, the determination of a mad world that's not listening.

If you fight for being right, you'll end up with shite and plight.

Instead, can you ease into the possibility that you are not in control? For a moment, consider the possibility that your small vision is no match for the grander vision your story holds. Consider the possibility of just going with that idea. This is not giving up. It is giving in to the Greater Wisdom that's just a whisper's shadow from your sight-line. You may never quite see it but you know it's there ... always.

You may never know your full story till you get to the last 1,000 words. That's not unusual. It's weird and scary but it's not unusual.

You may never know, as you sit to write every day, where the next 100, 1,000 or 5,000 words will take you. In fact, when I started this chapter, I had planned to write something quite different ... then these words turned up.

Are you scared? Fearful?

So, Mr or Mrs Perfectionist, start with opening yourself to the possibility that you're scared. Open yourself to the possibility that you're dreaming, conceiving or incubating a baby that might not turn out as you planned. What child does? Yes, take a moment to breathe into that.

Stop. And. Breathe.

Then say to yourself, "Yes, I'm frightened to let my child out of the house. He might trip over. She might upset people. They might not like him. They might criticise her flaws. They might ignore her ..." or whatever fear you may have for your precious child. Watch that fear as if it's dancing about on your open hand. It is not you. It is something you have and, like your phone or watch, you can put it down when it's reached its use-by date. Observe its frantic, frenzied flapping. Just see it writhing around, as if on your hand, and ask yourself if you really need it any more.

If you still need the fear, grasp it and don't let it go. You can let it go tomorrow or any other time you choose.

If you don't need it, watch it dissolve into the sunrise and enjoy a very different day.

Are you in control?

Having made a decision on the fear, either way, breathe into another possibility ... the possibility that you aren't in control. Breathe into the possibility that you have never been in control and, most critical of all, you have survived! Yes, despite an untidy life that won't obey your every expectation, you're here. You're okay. You're doing life as capably and as clumsily as the next person. It's untidy, it's out of control, you're still on a spinning orb hurtling through space at 66,600 miles an hour and you're still doing life okay.

And the same for your story. Despite its messiness, its out-of-controlness, it's still beckoning to you to start or continue writing. It still wants the particular road, motor and fuel you've graced it with. It chose you and it still wants you. It's waiting patiently.

So, sit down and do messy. Do random. Do unexpected. Let the story speak to you.

You, the road, will keep it on track – taking care of spelling, grammar, story structure and making sense. You, the motor, will give it a particular voice. You, the fuel, will keep it growing and stretching every day you sit down to write.

You do your bit and the story will do its bit – untidily, fearlessly and oh so beautifully.

Let it in and it'll let you out.

I'm a Procrastinator

I'm good at starting projects but not finishing them

Firstly, you are not a procrastinator. You are holding onto procrastination, but it is not you. Like a weightlifter holding up the barbells, you can drop it any time you like.

See, you are a human. You cannot change that. You cannot change your gender, height, birthplace, family, past, eye colour and a dozen other things about you. These things you cannot change as they are what you are.

What we can change are our attitudes, reactions and emotions.

"I am depressed …" No, you're doing depression. You can not-do it.

"I am peeling an orange …" Yes, you can stop when you like.

"I am a procrastinator …" No, you're doing procrastination and you can not-do it.

"I am cleaning my teeth …" Yes, you can stop when you like.

Also, you're holding onto the grenade of procrastination because you are scared.

Stop. And. Breathe.

Take that in. You are scared, just as every other human is.

This story, this book, is a part of you. You're birthing a

precious, fragile infant into a critical and uncaring world.

No.

Your infant is not fragile. It will survive the slings and arrows. The truth is that you think you won't survive the slings and arrows. But you will.

Several studies have asked people to rate the things they'd most fear doing. In every study, most put public speaking ahead of dying ... they would rather die than speak and face the judgement of others!

It seems we're genetically programmed to be approved of by everyone ... being "nice", agreeing with everyone, not saying no, emptying our souls to satisfy the needs of others.

So, welcome to the human race. We all fear judgement and not being enough.

And, you know what? You're not good enough. You'll never be good enough.

How do I know? Like you, we all have higher expectations of ourselves than others. We're harder on ourselves than everyone else!

If your pet dog or cat is sick, you'll rush off to the vet, immediately, do what needs to be done and spend money that needs to be spent. However, if you're sick, you'll probably tough it out, refuse to take time out, take yourself to work and not spend the necessary money to heal. Got that? We treat our pets better than we treat ourselves!

We treat our family and friends better than we treat ourselves.

Why are we that stupid? Because we're never good enough in our own eyes, in our own expectations. Because we're never good enough, because we're "misbehaving", we beat ourselves up for it. We push ourselves down to raise others up.

Once we recognise this, we have the choice to let it go. The weight of the barbells is asking us to let them down. But letting them down may not happen immediately – though it could – so, don't beat yourself up for not being an instant hero. An instant shero. An instant saint.

Philip J Bradbury

Just stay with the possibility that your not-good-enough is holding you back from finishing your project.

Just sit with it.

Just observe it.

Just smile as you watch it squirm and whinge under the spotlight of your new awareness.

Be patient. Be kind. You deserve patience and kindness. Then allow the procrastination to dissolve, day by day, as you approach the end of your novel.

Just turn up at the page and write like no one is watching … for no one is watching!

As you sit with your not-looking-good and not-good-enough and keep writing, the book will rise as the fear shrinks and, soon, you'll just have nothing but a book … finished!

Aiming for One Thing, Getting Something Else

I never seem to achieve my goals

Most people aim for nothing and hit it with amazing accuracy. Despite knowing that targets and goals move us forward, we resist them like price rises. Obviously, goals don't always get us to where we planned to be. In fact, they hardly ever do which does not prove they're useless.

Often they'll get us near to where we want to be and, having got there, we realise that's not where we want to be. The goal was wrong but helpful.

Jan, who attended one of my workshops, had been enduring a bitter divorce and a disturbing custody battle over her son. Wanting to find resolution to her particular problem, I encouraged her to set her sights wider and imagine what it would mean to her to help all children in custody battles. She eventually set a goal of becoming a divorce lawyer. Then she did her research and decided, dejectedly and eventually, that it would take too long, be too expensive and mean too much time away from her son. Wondering what to do next while feeling she'd failed the goal she had set herself, she had a call from a lady she'd met during her investigations into being a lawyer. It was a job offer and she's now working in the court system as a mediator in divorce cases and as an advocate for children in custody battles.

That connection, phone call and job would not have happened if she'd not set a goal that didn't seem to work. She's very happy her dream, her goal, did not come to fruition!

Though goals may seem to fail us – as per Jan's example – they do, primarily, get us moving in one direction or another. It's easier to steer a boat when it's moving. The same with us. If we're sitting on the couch, watching television and wondering what to do, it's unlikely that God will scream at us with a message of hope while handing us a gift-wrapped life.

All of our lives, all of the time, are works in progress and only by taking a step somewhere, anywhere, can we know if it's a right or a wrong one. From one step we'll get a feeling about the next and so on. As Martin Luther King Jnr said, "Just take the first step. You don't need to see the whole staircase. Just take the first step."

A goal sets a direction and a movement today, from what we know today. As we step forth, learning and experiencing new things, we can confirm or change our original goal.

By the way, before I started writing this article, I had the first sentence in my head and a strong idea of what I'd write about. However, after I wrote down that first sentence, my pen took off in a completely different direction and a totally different tribe of words emerged. And I'm still proud of the ones that turned up.

So, I challenge you: set a goal, take a step and remain open and excited about what the second step might be. If not today, then when?

Persistence

There is so much competition, I won't succeed

When I started writing seriously (not just for fun but with the intention to be published) I discovered that there are around 5,000 new books published in the USA every month – 60,000 a year. And that's just one country. If we add in all the books from Poland, Brazil, Australia, Germany, India, Iran, China and every other country, we're going to have quite a few books a year – something approaching a grazillion books a year. Then, added to that, are the 15 heptagrazillion books already published – that people are still reading – and we have something over 35 metaheptagrazillion books out there ... and the pile is getting bigger by the minute!

Then think of how long books have been published so far ... the earliest printed book is the Diamond Sutra, printed in China in 868 CE. In 1041, movable clay type was first invented in China. Johannes Gutenberg, a goldsmith and businessman from the mining town of Mainz in southern Germany, borrowed money to invent the printing press with replaceable/moveable wooden or metal letters in 1436 (completed by 1440).

So, given the length of time printing has been going on and how many books a year are printed, the number of books out there must be nearly a fraptillion - that's a word I made up for a really, really big number.

I was overwhelmed. What is the chance of standing out in

that crowd, huh? Actually, the odds are a metaheptagrazillion to one – not good odds at all.

The publishing industry – our brothers-in-arms – does writers no favours. All you'll hear is the high percentage of manuscripts that are turned down by publishers, the high percentage of published books that don't sell, the huge numbers of writers who have to keep their day jobs. The publishing industry – our fellow authors and the people who rely on us for their income – all want to tell you about the failures in the industry.

"Yes," they will say, "there are Agatha Christies, Stephen Kings, John Grishams, Paulo Coelhos and many other wildly successful authors but most are not wildly successful. In fact, most (at this point they're hinting that most = 99.9%) writers cannot make a living from writing."

At the time, some 15 years ago, I thought, "Well, someone's got to rise to the top. Why not me?" And so I kept writing and being turned down and writing and being turned down and writing … and eventually, I have eighteen books published and available on Amazon, Smashwords and IngramSparks. I may never have the income of Jilly Cooper or Richard Bach, from my writing, but it serves my soul (I cannot not write) and it helps serve my body.

I write for two reasons:
1. My soul demands it, gently and sweetly, and
2. My ego yearns to live by my writing income.

You see, in every writer there are stories to be told and if they are not released on paper, they become fetid and die smelly, making the writer bitter and sad. Letting these stories out gives us release, refreshment and it gives them light and life. Why would you deny light and life to your unborn stories?

Also, for every story written there is a reader awaiting. So why would you deny the reader(s) their pleasure? It can take some time to find those readers and patience and persistence is required. After ten years of trying to become an acknowledged and published musician, Bob Dylan had a hit song. A reporter asked him what it was like to be an overnight success. He smiled wryly and said something about ten years being a long "overnight".

The only real answer to your qualms about being published is simply to keep doing what you cannot not do – it will stop you becoming bitter and sad and, who knows, if you keep at it, you could become an overnight success!

Some examples of persistence (from my book *Dactionary*) may help to inspire you:

- Leon Uris, author of the bestseller *Exodus*, failed high school English three times.
- In 1962, four nervous young musicians played their first record audition for the executives of the Decca Recording Company. While turning down this British rock group called the Beatles, one executive said, "We don't like their sound. Groups of guitars are on the way out."
- In the 1940s, a young inventor, Chester Carlson, took his idea to 20 corporations, including some of the biggest in the country. They all turned him down. In 1947, after seven long years of rejections, he finally got a tiny company in Rochester (the Haloid Company), New York, to purchase the rights to his electrostatic paper-copying process. Haloid became Xerox Corporation, and both it and Carlson became very wealthy.
- When Pablo Casals reached 95, a young reporter asked him: "Mr. Casals, you are 95 and the greatest cellist who ever lived. Why do you still practice six hours a day?" Mr. Casals answered, "Because I think I'm making progress."
- Wilma Rudolph was the 20th of 22 children. She was born prematurely and her survival was doubtful. When she was 4 years old, she contracted double pneumonia and scarlet fever, which left her with a paralyzed left leg. At age 9, she removed the metal leg brace she had been

dependent on and began to walk without it. By 13 she had developed a rhythmic walk, which doctors said was a miracle. That same year she decided to become a runner. She entered a race and came in last. For the next few years every race she entered, she came in last. Everyone told her to quit, but she kept on running. One day she actually won a race. And then another. From then on she won every race she entered. Eventually this little girl, who was told she would never walk again, went on to win three Olympic gold medals.

- Louis L'Amour, successful author of over 100 western novels with over 200 million copies in print, received 350 rejections before he made his first sale. He later became the first American novelist to receive a special congressional gold medal in recognition of his distinguished career as an author and contributor to the nation through his historically based works.

So, now, do you think it's worth giving up?

The Persistence Of Paulo Coelho

The story of a story-man who didn't give up

Paulo Coelho is one of my favourite writers. I haven't read all his books and I haven't enjoyed every one I've read. In fact, I don't agree with many of the things he has written. There are, however, two things I like about him:

Firstly, his writing. He tries to weave personal and spiritual growth messages into his stories – not text books or non-fiction books but interesting novels. That's what I try to do.

Secondly, I like him as a man as he never gave up. Ever since he was a wee bitty lad he wanted to be, in his words, "a writer who is read and respected worldwide". He got there but it was one mammoth struggle.

Paulo suffered incarceration in mental homes by his parents, torture and imprisonment at the not-so-gentle hands of the Brazilian police and he chose to live it all through the fog of massive and continuous doses of drugs, nicotine, black magic, rejection and a multitude of relationships. Despite the myriad self-imposed and other distractions, he kept his eye on the page and, eventually, smiled to see over 100,000,000 of his books sold around the world.

I don't know if the achievement of his dream has made him happier but he did it – he set a target and he hit it … and he continues to write, to the delight of his millions of fans.

Writing is not like welding, teaching or nursing where you get a qualification, find a job and live happily ever after.

With writing, there is no school that will give you the most important skills of persistence, persistence and bloody persistence ... and a rhino skin to deflect all those rejection slips. No school anywhere in this universe can give you that. It's got to come from inside you and no one can show you where inside it sits. That's your job to find it and you usually find it (or not) when that first rejection slip arrives – you're either flattened by it and then you start running and stop writing forever or it enrages and emboldens you to write more furiously, more creatively, more plaintively or more beautifully. However you write, that rejection slip will get you writing more of it, if you choose.

If you find that tiny compartment in your brain (or wherever you keep it) marked Bloody Persistence and Thick Skin and you get it out and use it, you'll probably succeed.

However, the really difficult part is that no one on this good earth can tell you when all that persistence and thick skin will pay off. You see, it would be so easy if someone told you that, if you keep writing and writing and writing and submitting and submitting and submitting you will be accepted by a publisher in twelve years' time. You'd just plan your life, get a day-job for twelve years, get writing and submitting for those twelve years and then you'd be in writing heaven.

But it doesn't work like that – we're not welders, teachers or nurses. We start writing and we have no idea if it will be two, five, twelve, twenty or thirty years before we get that magic Yes from an agent or publisher. It could be today, tomorrow or never ... we never know from one day to the next.

For Paulo Coelho it was about thirty years and, along the way, there were many near-misses – times when he thought he'd hit the target only to find his hopes dashed again. So, up he'd get and write some more.

And that's what I admire about him and that, above all

else, is probably why he can write about personal and spiritual growth so eloquently – he's been there and done it.

Walking My Talk and Remembering

I keep regretting my inaction but still can't get going

Depression, it seems, is difficult to detect when you're in the middle of it. But, as you start to climb out of it, you can look back and say, "Aah, so there was I." Over the last 20 years I have written at least 1,000 words, most days. However, over the last 3 months I have written nothing. Not a word. Then, last week, I started writing again and I can look back and say, "Aah, so there was I."

I had betrayed myself in two ways.

I had betrayed myself, firstly, for giving up on my passion. I forgot who I was and what I was here for. I let the dream slip through my fingers and crumble into the dust from which I crafted it. I lost my reason and I lost myself.

Secondly, I betrayed myself because I did not walk my talk. Here I am telling writers to turn up at the page, be persistent, accept judgement, deal with the bitch on your shoulder, keep writing even when you are empty of words and when you've lost the desire to write anything. Keep writing, one word at a time, even when it's hardest to write … especially when it's hard to write!

I should have given that advice to myself – I needed it and

I rejected it.

I didn't know what was hardest – giving up and living with the regret or keeping going when it's just too hard. I've now tried both and giving up is harder. This is the single hardest day of my life and I really, really, really don't want to write. I just want to curl up and cry and hope the world would go away and stop being so hard … to stop rejecting me.

But, now I've tasted the sourness of regret, I don't want that more than anything else in the world. So my rusty pen begins to move again, creaking and resisting each word, reluctant to start yet another line. It aches to curl up and die but it aches even more to avoid the rancid stench of regret. And so it moves through another sentence, becoming less scratchy, less reluctant, less regretful with every sweep and loop.

Like someone jumping from a sinking ship, thrashing the water to avoid being sucked down by the disappearing hulk, I fight and claw and scream for life. With every stroke I'm a millimetre further from death and a millimetre closer to life. As the regret sinks away and I continue to fight for hope, the struggle becomes gradually easier. Each word saves me for the next and I begin to lose the panic and feel the ease. It gets easier and I'm not giving up. I now see land ahead and so my strokes take me not from the death of regret but to a life of purpose.

And how did I find myself in this sorry state?

I used to be what the world calls successful. I was married with two amazing children. I had a prestigious job, a four-bedroom house in an expensive suburb, two cars, a boat and money for lots of hobbies. But I was out of love with myself and my life. I hated accounting and was bored stiff. In fact, I had been bored with it for most of the 18 years I'd done it. I'd continually asked God for deliverance and, eventually, a quiet and reassuring voice asked me to leave it all behind and follow my passion. I obeyed, threw myself into the shiny new world of New Age, started publishing other peoples' books, started writing for magazines and I was instantly fulfilled. I was told I should get my own writings published and, after rejections from every publisher in New Zealand (and some in Australia), I published my own books. I sold a few but never enough to live on and I worked part-time as a lecturer to keep body and soul together. My teaching took me to Australia and South Africa with personal development and AIDS workshops. I became editor of a New Age magazine and then, with my partner, Anna, bought a loss-making, provincial newsletter and turned it into a paid, national magazine ... which flopped rather sadly.

When you're down, there's no point in getting up and doing what you've always done. You've got to get up and do something differently ... or the same thing in a different way. We decided to do what we'd always wanted to do and had never done – live in England and experience Europe for a few years. We got "real" jobs, paid our debts off, built up some savings, got married and set off for merrie Englande.

In the 49 months I was in England, I worked for 29 of them. I lost five jobs and had around 200 job applications rejected. Amid all that, I wrote my first novel, The Last Stand Down, and had it rejected by 19 writers agents.

I might laugh at or minimise each failure, each rejection, but they all hurt. Each one seems small at the time but they all go right in and they do not leave. They build up so subtly, so sneakily, that we don't realise the heavier and heavier load of failure we're carrying inside us. Our muscles grow stronger to enable us to hold up the load but, eventually, it's too much.

My last "rejection" was losing my job at Azad University when it closed down. No, it wasn't my fault that the university collapsed and, no, it was not a rejection of me. But it went in, it hurt and it was the one that I eventually collapsed under.

Making an occupation (an unpaid one) of sending out job applications, it took me some time to realise I had not been writing. I then thought about it a lot and the idea held a lot of fear ... fear that every word I committed to paper opened yet another opportunity for rejection.

I'd stopped writing and now I've started again. The fear of rejection has not gone but it is fading as I acknowledged, openly to myself, the pain that it caused. Facing my demons, my fears, has brought them into the light where they cannot scare me so much. They may take some time to dissolve – or they may never go – but calling each one out of the line, by name, diminishes their power. And, as their power fades, so does my dream, my passion come forth. The fear of success transforms, word by word, into the glory of success.

Since I returned to my writing, I had an invitation to attend a three-day writer's conference in London – for free! Then, yesterday, I met a friend who reminded me of myself – she encouraged me back to the dream I'd left behind … and that's what happens when we return – we stop dismembering ourselves and we start remembering.

Then, somehow, I ended up in Australia. And, somehow, I met Jeff and, weirdly, we ended up rewriting The Last Stand Down as a stage play and recorded it as a podcast … with the big, hairy goal of having it taken up as a film.

I don't know how long it will take to reach the dry land of hope and life but I've left the sinking vessel of regret behind. It can no longer drag me down. So I write another word … and another … and smile.

Questions Are More Powerful Than Answers

How do I conquer writer's block?

Oh how I love a blank, white page; a void, a nothingness, on which to allow the magic of words to fall. There is nothing so glorious as the emptiness of potential, of the anticipation of the unexpected. And how much more refreshing is a question than an answer.

An answer is the end of all things, the place where creativity stops and there is no more. I am a carpenter … I am a doctor … I am an asthmatic … I am depressed … I am happy … what do you do with those answers? Oh that's nice for you … Oh dear, you poor thing … and the conversation ends. Answers are predictable and certain, like actors reading their scripts.

How different, then, when asked, "Who/what are you?" to have your answer a question. I am just pondering that myself … If answers were tears, I'd be happy … I am the question you've been waiting for … I am you in a holy encounter with myself.

Most of us baulk at uncertainty but that is the juice of all artists and art.

Not everyone basks in the security of tried and true. Most feel a deep loneliness in the Vale of Intangibility. There are some other souls – small in number and big in heart – who sunbathe naked on the Mount of Mystery and float freely in the Sea of Synchronicity. They expose themselves to whatever comes their way, blissfully charmed to give up control and let what will be, be. Armed with nought but their anticipation of a New Secret to be revealed, they wake to each day as if it were a beautifully wrapped gift. They rise from sleep with a smile on their lips, a bounce in their step and the joy of opening yet another glorious mystery from the God of Adventures.

They work the same ordinary jobs, shop the same cloistered shopping centres, drive the same winding roads and walk the same grey streets other folks do. Their outer skin is the same as yours and mine but their inner world is as different as chalk and peas.

They seem, somehow, to find out about fun stuff at work before others do, to accidentally receive free gifts we miss out on, to find a more memorable road to travel and a lighter path to tread. They seem to have a constant smile, have a greater interest in what you and I do and remember it all so much better than you and I do.

So many of us take out insurance, set burglar alarms and raise defences in our lives and minds to protect ourselves from evil ... and yet bad things still happen. Certainty is an illusion.

However, the minds of us feckless and reckless ones are blank, white pages, ready to receive whatever comes to us. And, mysteriously, our defencelessness and our uncontrolling manner lets in the good stuff. Unable (or unwilling) to filter and arrange our lives, we keep the pages open with gleeful anticipation, allowing only the gleeful to fall on them.

The question without an answer allows only beautiful synchronicity to heed its call.

As I sat with my coffee and carrot cake in this shopping centre, full of humanity's noise and drama, I held nothing but glee at seeing these blank, white pages. I had no control or intention and whatever words have fallen from my pen ... well, they've done nothing but add gleefulness to my glee. Whoopee!

P.S. I packed my pen and paper away and, as I drank the last of my coffee, I saw not a blank, white coffee cup bottom but a huge painted smiley face chuckling back at me.

P.P.S. As I left the car park, anticipating the parking fee of $4.00, I discovered that the rain had meddled with the debit card machine and they let me out for free!

On the blank, white page a smile is writ ... always! :-)

Why Do I Choose Failure?

I give up easily - how do I keep going?

A Course in Miracles tells us that the course (itself) is both simple and difficult to do.

Its simplicity is that all we are asked to do is change our minds about everything and everyone in our lives – from fear to love, judgement to acceptance, anger to peace, hate to liking. Simple.

The difficult part is that we must do it in every moment of our lives; with every event and every person we come across – people at work, on TV, on the bus, in our homes, in our dreams … every single person and event. It is difficult to maintain that consistency of thought, that diligence of direction, and we appear to forget. However, the course tells us that we do not forget. We consciously choose not to remember because we fear the benefits of changing our minds: we are afraid of our light, we fear the greatness we are and we stop ourselves losing the fear and judgement that we have identified with for so long. We consciously hold ourselves back from our greatest potential because we're more comfortable in our littleness, our self-pity and our pain. Fearing the discomfort of being bigger, we 'forget'.

On a Linkedin forum, recently, a writer said he had started his first novel but he was unhappy with the beginning. Having written some way past the beginning, he didn't want to continue until he got the beginning right. He wanted to know how he could improve the beginning so he could continue with the rest of the story.

I suggested he forget the beginning and just keep writing, allowing the beginning to take care of itself – it could be changed at any time and a better one would probably present itself as he continued with the rest of the story.

He's no different from the rest of us who find ourselves progressing in some area of our lives (relationships, career, finances, health, etc.) and that progress becomes fearful:

What if I don't have these complaints any more? Who will I be then?

What if I don't have this poverty any more? Who will I be then?

What if I don't have this struggle any more? Who will I be then?

What if I'm finally a published author? Who will I be then?

We find some small, irrelevant detail to focus on, something that must be 'fixed' before we can continue, something that holds us back from the uncomfortable light and greatness that we are.

I'm currently writing a novel and have writers block. I can't see where the story should go next so I asked my wife to read the 20,000 words I've written it to see if she had any ideas. Being busy at the moment, she hasn't got around to doing this and so I've stopped ... I then realised I'm using her non-reading as my excuse not to carry on.

There is power in movement, in starting and continuing. You can't steer a stationary ship and God can only steer us to our rightful goals when we get up steam, whatever the weather and the seas.

I know I don't forget. I know I choose to hold myself back and, knowing that, I find it easier to move forward and to experience miracles. I know that I don't always move in the right direction but, if I keep moving forward – in any direction – the right one opens before me.

Apple Cider, Doing It Badly And Writing

I keep being diverted by things - how do I stay on track?

In Oxfordshire, we'd been making apple cider while learning about life and writing.

Making apple cider is hard work and, at the end of a hot summer's day the three of us smell … well, let's just say, fecund … we feel like we've carried donkeys across the Sahara and we probably look like Arnold Schwarzenegger, after a hard day's mayhem.

Picking apples from the ground is easy enough thought the buckets are heavy to carry the hundred yards to the old, brick shed. Cutting the apples into quarters is easy enough, for the first two thousand, and then the hard work starts. Bucket by bucket, the chopped apples are poured into the spout of the press and someone has to turn the handle to squash them through the mincer. They don't go willingly! Just think of the power one needs to exert into one bite of an apple, especially a hard one, and now multiply that by a thousand, for six hours on end.

Then, having forced them through the gnashing teeth of the grinder, by strong arm, into the round, wooden, slatted press, one then has to squeeze the bejeezers … well, juice, actually … out of them. This is done by winding down a massive thumb-screw till they all collapse into an exhausted heap and give up their clear, life-blood into our eagerly waiting container. The turning of the screw, my darlings, is no easy feat – apples do not surrender easily and it's a whole-body experience to exert several tons of pressure on a tribe of quietly screaming apples. When they've succumbed, we unwind the screw, pour in more quarters, turn the grinder, wind down the thumb-screw, unwind ... and, once in a while, carry a massive bucket of exhausted apple pulp the hundred yards to the compost heap and then enjoy the sunshine as we pick another 73,000 tons of apples ... no, actually, it's a bucket or two but it feels like more and more as the day progresses.

That's the start of making apple cider and we all slept an exhausted – more exhausted than the apples – and happy sleep as our muscles unknotted themselves and smiled again.

And life? Aah, yes, the revelations on life. Well, as Suzie was turning the screw with grimace and furrowed brow, I offered to relieve her.

She said, "If you want to do something, even if you do it badly, NEVER GIVE UP!" She stopped and smiled wistfully. "My God, you never forget the things your parents taught you and that was my father's favourite phrase – even if you do it badly, NEVER GIVE UP! And I can't, it's so ingrained." Then she returned to squishing apples into submission.

A Course in Miracles (ACIM) is a psychological/spiritual course to help us experience abiding peace and joy, irrespective of the events and dramas around us. It tells us that doing the course and achieving the results is both easy and difficult. The steps to take, the changing our minds about ourselves and others, are very simple steps – you need no degrees, no rituals, no money and anyone of any age or creed can do it. The difficult part is that we have to do it in every second of our lives. Every time a negative thought, a thought of judgement or a peace-less feeling comes to us, we acknowledge it and change it to one of peace.

Initially, of course, being totally present to my thoughts, in every moment, was difficult. In fact, my mind could wander off and wallow in self-pity or anger for days. I did the ACIM process very badly but I kept doing it. As I became more vigilant, I would notice that my mind enjoyed taking the detours into thoughts of revenge, victimhood or sarcasm. I kept doing it, very, very badly and, as I kept doing it I could hold my mind in place for whole seconds, then minutes, then hours at a time. I have a long way to go till I get to that constant state of wakefulness but, as I keep doing it badly, I keep getting better.

The same is true of writing. I come across great writers who write badly. Some continue doing it badly and end up with truly great work. Others stop at the doing it badly stage, thinking they're not good writers.

It's like tying our shoes or buttoning a shirt, which we are all capable of doing, eventually. As small children we do those things badly but we insist on continuing. Then we learn to ride a bike (badly), learn to read (badly), learn to drive a car (badly), learn to interact with the opposite sex (badly) and operate a bank account (badly). Doing it badly can be frustrating and/or fearful but we end up doing each of those things very well. However, they are the basic, practical things of life and there's no question we'll succeed ... because we really want to!

In some things we're not sure of success. The doubt creeps in and we are apt to blame parents, teachers and everyone else. We begin to doubt ourselves.

We may realise we have a flair for writing (or painting, gymnastics, statistics or whatever) and do it badly. Then the doubter – yes, that bitch constantly on your shoulder – shouts in your left ear that you're useless, you'll never make it and it's best you stop right now before you make a fool of yourself in front of others ... others who have their own little doubters screaming abuse in their ears.

ACIM tells us that we don't forget to take the steps to attaining lasting peace and contentment. Rather, we don't do them because we believe we don't deserve the results.

The same with writing or any other skill – we do not persevere because we do not believe we deserve the rewards of a job not-badly done ... of a successful career in our chosen field.

That's the reason I started my publishing company – I'm not disenchanted with the publishing industry (as most new publishers seem to be) but I know how hard it is to constantly do things badly till I do them better. I know about the bitch on my shoulder and I know about the feelings of underservedness ... and I also know how great you and I really are.

Feel free to send me your manuscript (or what you've done of it) and I will tell you what you must continue to do (badly), what you're doing brilliantly – yes, there will be something you're doing brilliantly – and how to replace the doubter with the abiding sense of peace from which all great work flows.

That, my friend, is my sacred mission – let me help you and I'll know more of peace as I sip my excellent apple cider ... the pen-ultimate reward!

Creative Spaces

I can't write where and when others tell me to

Expecting consistency from me is like a porcupine expecting silence at a balloon party. It's just not going to happen.

You see, I have preached about creating quietness and space around you to enable your muses to speak. However, as I recall, I wrote those sermons in a noisy, busy city cafés in the middle of shopping centres!

"So, what's the deal, huh?" I hear you ask. "You don't practice what you preach!"

No I don't. Guilty as accused, your honour. Let me clarify what a sacred space of writing really is – it is whatever you deem it to be. So there!

A few years ago, while fully employed as a lecturer, I wrote most of my book, Whose Life Is It Anyway? Each morning I'd wake with a chapter heading in my head and, over breakfast, I'd pour my thoughts onto paper. Thankfully, my wife was tolerant of my inattention to her at those times. I was keen to finish the book and felt that, if I didn't have to work, I'd get it finished quicker. My wife agreed to me taking a year off work – did I mention she was very tolerant? During that intended year of writing, I hardly did anything on the book. Without the structure of a regular job, I did lots of things but few of them helped to finish the book. After many months I realised I was wasting my time and my wife was becoming considerably less tolerant as I had so little to show for my great write-fest. I went back to work and, pow!, the book was finished within a month and on bookshelves the following month.

Another seventeen books later, I look back and realise most of my writing has been in noisy cafés. For me, taking myself off to some remote and lonely place does not work. Well, to date it hasn't. I wish it did then I would go to some romantically remote and lonely place and churn out the book of everybody's dreams. It seems that the more distractions I have, the better. I'd like it to be different but, right now, it isn't.

Stephen King is much more disciplined than I am and has a regular regime of writing from early to mid-morning ... every single day.

Paulo Cuelho writes solidly – almost twenty four hours a day – for two weeks every two years. And then he rests from his labours for 102 weeks.

My friend, David Gaughan, wrote The Blue Star between 11.00 pm and 4.00 am, over a year, while holding down a full-time day job.

There are as many different sacred writing spaces as there are writers. The trick for us is to find the situation in which our creativity grows best. It might be regular, disciplined writing sessions or it might be more random and unexpected bouts of manic outpourings. It might be in an isolated mountain cave or it might be on a bus, where I also did lots of my writing. It might be morning or evening. It might be when there's nothing else to think about or it may be during the micro-breaks in a frantic schedule.

What works for one writer won't be what works for others and the system you find (or stumble upon) probably won't suit anyone else. Just as the combination of your history, culture, experience, qualifications and dreams is unique, so is the way you express your creativity. Maybe you write better on a hot beach or maybe you write better when it's raining. Perhaps it's better when you're happy or maybe when you're stressed and/or sad.

Maybe you write best after alcohol or maybe it's best after you purify your body and imbibe only pure water.

What works for you is what works for you so don't feel frustrated because you can't write effectively under someone else's regime. Experiment with what could bring on that great book of yours and try to connect with spaces and situations you feel most at home with.

When you're in the zone, the writing is easier and more beautiful to read so please, please, please don't succumb to anyone else's need for you to do it their way. We need your unique creativity and that can only come from your unique way of doing it.

So, go and experiment and let those beautiful words out ... now!

Accepting Judgement

I don't think I can deal with the criticism I'll get for my book

What does WRITE stand for? Wisdom Risking Itself To Exposure.

There are two main reasons that writers ... well, anyone, really ... do not step up to the line of their passion and power – judgement and overwhelming odds.

My father wrote a moving and fascinating book about his career, running a 22,000-acre sheep and cattle station. I typed it up and encouraged him to send it to several publishers. He sent it to one publisher who turned it down and that was the end of it – it was never seen again and my father would never talk of it again.

Most artists live life in a quandary – they dearly want their art exposed to and shared by the world and yet they fear the judgement of the world. Like my father, so many writers crawl back into their sensitive shells at the first sniff of criticism, the first hint of a suggestion that their writing could be improved in some way.

The only writers who are successful are the thick-skinned ones, the courageous ones, the ones who know some people will not like their work. Chicken Soup for the Soul, by Jack Canfeld and Mark Victor Hansen, was turned down 140 times. Yet, when it was eventually published, it sold over 80 million copies!

Sir Laurence Olivier, one of the greatest actors of all time, said that if he did not get stage fright his performance would be a poor one. Stage fright got his pulse racing, his adrenalin flowing and his mind focused. So, even great performers live in fear and trepidation, every single performance ... and they keep going. In fact, the fear helped make Sir Laurence great.

J.D. Salinger, who wrote the American classic, Catcher In The Rye, could not deal with the massive and positive acclaim of his great novel. He stopped writing and spent the rest of his life in seclusion. He was a great writer who wanted to write more but who could not deal with the judgement – a talent wasted, we might say.

So, you may enjoy the quiet solitude as you write your great novel but, one day, gentle writer, you will have to face the madding crowd and the judgement of others. That judgement may be condemnation or acclaim and, in the battleground of the heart, they are equally daunting.

You may create the classic of the century but if no one reads it, it is nothing but scrap paper. You are not on this earth for nothing – if you have a yearning to write you probably have a talent for it. Please, please, please do not retreat into your sensitive shell – feel the stage fright and know that some will love your words and some will hate them. Write your words, get them out there and be proud of what you've done. Let the cards fall where they will and know that, if you're stirred by your writing, at least one other person will be. If you change just one person's life, your mission is complete. Well done!

Wisdom And Words From The Silence

Most of us listen to the outer world and it's not always nice

Listening is not something that comes to us naturally. We are not taught to listen to our inner world and so it must come to us when we're not looking, not trying. Only when we realise we do not need to write from our own strength, from our own imagination, do words come more easily. As we tap into that greater strength and imagination by the effortless merging with silence, we discover the real reason we're here and what we have to share with a noisy world.

The following is my first experience of the power of silence, the power of listening, and is in my book, *My Whispering Teachers*.

Sitting by the sea is a lonely experience – an experience of the smooth grey sand stretching and curving for miles away on either side, an experience of the wet black rocks buffeted by the waves forever in time, an experience of the swaying desolate sea stretching beyond the horizon and an experience of the sky, only blue nothingness, forever in space. Expanses of flat blue and grey with rugged lumps of black. Forever stillness beyond vision and time. I seem to be the only being on this planet – not a footprint, a voice or a being to break the monotony of the flat unending nothingness.

So, what's the point of my being? Just to be amid this world of nothingness. No food from the sand or water from the sea to nourish me. No sounds to stimulate, no sights to invigorate, no sensations to excite. Nothingness and emptiness.

Then from that sad and heavy question come a thousand answers. From where I know not for there are none to speak. But speak they do, in compassionate, loving and knowing tones.

"So there is someone here?" I wonder.

"There is always someone here," they say. "In every lonely place and every quiet space there are more around to help than in the busy streets and noisy parties."

"How can there be someone, anyone, here with all of this nothingness?" I wonder to myself.

"It is from the nothingness that everything is," comes the reply, firm and smiling, somehow. "Nothing is everything," they continue, "for in nothingness is nothing but the Self. And in the silence of the Self is everything there is."

"In the silence of myself ….." I muse. "Perhaps I had not stopped the noise to hear the silence of myself before."

"And why haven't you turned off the noise before?" they ask gently.

"Perhaps I have just been too busy," I answer.

"Or too afraid?" they ask.

"Afraid?" I wonder, disquieted. "Afraid of what?"

"Afraid of yourself," they answer. "Afraid of your silence, your nothingness."

My mind stops, goes blank. For a second that lasts forever I have no answer, no question, no thought at all. The stillness continues until I feel awkward and have to intrude.

"Why should I be afraid of the silence? It's not scary," I challenge.

"Then why did you have to move from it to ask that question?" they ask.

"How can I answer their question?" I wonder, searching for

answers. My mind goes blank and quiet. And peaceful. This stillness is new to me – new, nice but a little ... scary. Perhaps they are right.

"Why would I be afraid of this peaceful silence?" I ask myself.

They do not reply.

"Have you gone?" I ask, a little concerned.

"We are always here, Dear One," they reply with compassion. "We are always here where the silence and stillness is."

"Thanks," I say, relieved. Then I wonder about my relief – am I really that afraid of my aloneness?

"You see, we do not need to answer," they say. "In the stillness you have your own answers."

"O.K. just for argument's sake, if I am afraid, then why?" I query.

"Why are you afraid to truly admit your fear," they ask, gently.

This is becoming unsettling. I shuffle in the sand and look around. Still no one. Just me.

"Please don't be afraid," they say. "You forget that we are always here – holding your hand and guiding your heart."

I feel better but still worry about my fear. The worst thing is that I don't know what I am afraid of.

"Of yourself, of course," they say.

"Afraid of me?" I ask incredulously. "How can I be afraid of little, old me. I am me so how can I be afraid of that?"

"Fear only creeps in where there is no love," they answer.

"No love ... that's a heavy one," I muse.

"If you truly love yourself then you have no fear of being truly alone with yourself," they say.

"So I am afraid because I do not love myself?" I ask, a little worried. "I thought I was doing very well, having battled with low self-esteem, indecision and worry of what others thought of me for 40-odd years. I thought I was winning."

"You are winning and you have done extremely well," they

say with enthusiasm. "You have, for the first time, touched your silence and that is a major step. Congratulate yourself as we congratulate you."

"Thanks," I say, a little embarrassed. "But I only found this silence by accident. I never knew it was here, so how could I fear it?"

"Sorry, but there are no excuses," they reply. "You have always known it was here and that, in here, was you, the real you. You couldn't face it before but you can now. Well done!"

I smile and search for that space and silence again. It immediately overwhelms me with its peace and joy and tears flow from my eyes. "So what was there to be afraid of?" I ask.

"Nothing," they reply. "You have filled that space, your space, with love, and the fear has left, forever."

"I thought I had done so well in this life – so many achievements, so many friends, so many assets," I query to myself. "But none of those things have given me the contentment and joy I now feel. It's crazy. What was I looking for?"

"Remember you are a human 'being', not a human 'doing'," they say. "Your purpose is not to do, but to be and in the being, to be love."

"So why do we all try to 'do' all of the time?" I ask, confused.

"So that you can avoid the 'being'. You are all afraid of yourselves, afraid of the silence. Afraid of the fear that never is."

"So our only purpose here is to really love ourselves?" I ask, wondering at the simplicity.

"And as you love yourself, you can love others," they say. "As you love yourself, others will change before your eyes. You will see through the eyes of love rather than through the eyes of fear, as before. All will become brighter and more beautiful – people, animals, the sea, the sky, the sand …."

I look and the sea is smiling, sparkling. The sand scrunches and laughs, the sky warms my heart and the rocks frolic in the water.

"I am alive!" I yell and then immediately look around,

embarrassed, to see if anyone is here.

"There is always someone here," they say, smiling.

"Thank God there is only you at this moment," I think, "I could do with some peace and quiet!"

Isolation And Interaction – Writers Groups

I don't know any other writers and I need support

A writer's life is a lonely one – how many times have you heard that statement? Of course, it's not true, no matter how many times you hear it. A writer's life is as they choose to make it – lonely or not.

However, what is true is that a writer's work (which is part of her/his life) is a solo one. No one else can pick up your pen and move it across the page. No one else can press the buttons on the keyboard for you. No one else can think your thoughts or play in your imagination. No one else knows what you know. No one else can dip into that source of greater knowing for you – the greater knowing that creates the dance of your pen across the paper or the jig of keyboard chatter.

In all this creation and recreation (writing and rewriting) process you are totally alone and no one else can do that for you.

Being alone or solo are not the same thing as being lonely. Alone and solo are physical states – no one else is in our presence. Being lonely is a mental/emotional state and can be chosen in any physical state – with others or not.

As a writer, we must be able to savour our aloneness, to seek it out and to bathe in it with the gentle peace and joy born of the creative urge to write beautiful words.

However, you do not need to be alone all the time.

If we ever find aloneness lonely, if we hate the physical separation from others and rile against it every time we sit to write, we should not be writers. Some people just cannot be done with their own selves, their own thoughts, and must forever be in the melee of human interaction and drama. If you are one of these people, ever afraid of aloneness and stillness, then writing is not for you. Go and be a politician or something.

However, if you have a passion to write but can only bear aloneness for a part of your time, get writing. If you like to balance aloneness with interaction, you're in the majority of writers – welcome to the club!

There are, of course, writers who crave aloneness all the time. J D Salinger, writer of that American classic, Catcher in the Rye, could not deal with the massive, positive acclaim after his book was published and thereafter lived in seclusion. He wrote no more though there were many more books in him that he wished to write.

So, finding the balance seems to be the most healthy and productive way to write. If you're a new writer, sensitive about comments on your virginal work, the best place to start is to join a writers group. If there isn't one in your area, start one. No matter how experienced you are, you will be able to contribute to others' work by simply listening and helping them overcome their sensitivity to others' opinions.

Also, you never know where things can lead to when you communicate with another human. An example from my own experience:

A friend suggested it was time I wrote another song. I hadn't done that for a long time and, surprised by his suggestion, sat down to see what would emerge from my pen. A poem, The Wychwood Badgers Run, came out and I read it at the next meeting of the Chipping Norton Writers' Group. I'm not sure what happened next, out of my ear-shot, but I soon found myself being asked to recite the poem at a Woodland Festival and that led to me singing and playing guitar at the festival – something I'd always wanted to do. It was terrifying and deeply satisfying.

And, no, I didn't get a publishing contract from the experience but I will tell you this – and on this rock I stand – we need to move from our aloneness (at times) and to talk with others. When we do we open the door to endless, unimagined opportunities.

And, yes, it can be terrifying, mortifying and downright embarrassing to read your work out ... and not just for the first time. Writers who have been doing it forever can still feel confronted and uncomfortable when reading their words to an audience.

However, if you start with a writing group – people who are equally as embarrassed as you are – the strength of their support will give you wings to fly even higher. It's never a competition – everyone in writing groups (in my experience) just wants to support every other writer in the same measure that they want support from others.

So, choosing between aloneness and interaction can be a delicate balance. By choosing both – however you balance it – will give you wings. Happy flying!

Confessions of a Magazine Writer

Persistence, bloody persistence and unexpected magic

In July 1993, four days before his fortieth birthday, Sam Barton left his eighteen-year marriage. He left the woman he'd known for 25 years as his new life just didn't fit into a relationship that allowed no room for growth. No room for change.

You see, a few years previously, he'd studied Rudolf Steiner and, more recently had come across meditation, his psychic abilities and the whole nine yards of the New Age movement. His world had suddenly exploded into a massive new, unseen world ... an unseen world that was almost more real than the little tangible one he'd been standing on for thirty nine years.

Then he was introduced to the men's movement and his growing world got bigger still.

Along with this exciting, confusing and endlessly fascinating world, he rediscovered his writing ability – an ability he'd had at school but which had to take a back seat on his drive through qualifications, jobs, marriage, children and all the other trappings of getting ahead in this tangible world ... no, it had not taken a back seat, it had been tossed out to languish in the dust of his dash to progress. Then the world became bigger and all that stuff that had been so important before, as a child, awoke, dusted itself off and confronted him with a huge smile of recognition.

Once the cork was off the bottle, there was no putting the genie back. Sam began to be woken at silly times like five am with words rattling round in his head. Words that would keep him awake till he wrote them down. Words that could keep him distracted and irritable for days. Words that were fully formed sentences, fully formed articles. The sooner he wrote them down the better. Only then was there peace.

His only choice was when he wrote them down – not what he wrote down. He'd write them as they came out of his head but, as he typed them up, he'd sometimes feel the need to change them. Then he'd read his typewritten words and always, always, always, need to go back and reinstate the originally presented words and phrases. These words were as persistent as he was.

And so this outpouring started and it had nowhere to go. Sam discovered he was not one of those writers who was content to write stuff and have it sit in the drawer for no one else to see. He just had to get it published somehow. He didn't know how but started asking around. Then, mysteriously, three days after he started asking around, he found that the best New Age magazine in New Zealand was published right there in his home town of Tauranga. With that discovery came the instant knowing that he would write for that magazine. He didn't know how to do that, so asked again. A week later, at a New Age event, he was introduced to the publisher of this magazine.

A normally shy person, he surprised himself when the words fell out of his mouth, telling this publisher that all of the writers in her magazine were women and that it would expand her readership if she had a man writing for her. She was polite but not convinced. He took her contact details and said she would hear from him … and hear from him she did!

Every month, for the next year, he either phoned or emailed her with articles, article ideas and the benefits of having a male writer on board. A year later she succumbed to his relentlessness and accepted one article – an article that generated more letters to the editor than had all previous articles for the last five years. He was hired and wrote regularly for that magazine for five years. Then he became the editor. During that time, Sam sent his articles and ideas to magazines and became a regular writer for nine other magazines in New Zealand, Australia, South Africa and Czech Republic.

What Sam discovered was that the words were always there. If an editor wanted an article at short notice, he could rattle up 1,000 or 2,000 words within an hour ... as long as it was on subjects he was passionate about – personal growth, spiritual growth, men's issues and business. He was not an expert in any of those fields – a novice who dabbled, really – but when the words were needed, they always appeared in perfect formation. All he had to do was turn up at the page and let his pen loose. Usually, he had no idea of what was going to come out of the end of his pen and, as he wrote each article, he could never tell how it would end till it did. Mysteriously, the articles always ended at the right number of words – an editor would give him a word-count and the words would arrange themselves to fit that. It was intriguing but, somehow, it never surprised him.

One thing did surprise him, though: In his field of personal and spiritual development, there were no immutable laws, no fixed and immovable edicts to govern the field. Everything, absolutely everything, was opinion, based on what worked for one person. Timid, at first, at venturing his opinion, he discovered that the more outlandish, the more satirical, the more challenging were his articles, the more the readers liked them. He stopped being "nice" and became brave, venturing ideas and theories that went against the current thinking. People asked for more. People argued with him and told him he was wrong. People seemed to love it, whether they agreed with him or not. Perhaps, he surmised, people (like children) like or need something to hit against, need others to draw their lines in the sand for them. Perhaps that's why readers need writers to write articles for them. Maybe. Maybe not.

And now those articles are scattered amongst several of the books he's had published – Articles of Faith, Understanding Men, The Royal Bank of Stories, Conversations on Your Business and My Whispering Teachers.

[Sam Barton does not exist. Philip J Bradbury does. This is my story.]

The moral of the story is to seek what you want. Ask, ask and ask again . Though you may not feel you're the absolute expert on your subject/passion, the universe will chip in with its own wisdom when you leap off your cloud and pretend to fly … the moment you leap, you'll find you can fly, on the wings of a deeper wisdom you couldn't have been aware of before leaping.

So, happy leaping!

Are We There Yet?

I love writing but I don't want to write a whole book.

Writing a book is a long and glorious journey that gives immense satisfaction, especially when it's printed and in readers' hands.

But it is a long journey. No doubt about that. And, sometimes (oft-times!) it can seem never-ending, painful and hardly worth the daily grind for all those years.

Like any long journey with the kids moaning, "Are we there yet? Are we there yet?" it is a good idea to break the trip up, get out of the car and have some shorter experiences. For the writer, one of these can be our regular writing group where we actually get to see there's a world beyond our screen and our office window ... and to meet up with real, live in-the-flesh people as oddly passionate about writing as we are.

Another way to break the trip up is to enter writing competitions. They challenge us to break out of our daily style and try something new and scary – something not quite us. This can invigorate our current writing project and bring a freshness to it. They also give us a quicker result and, sometimes, a quicker reward – money and fame. I have a Facebook page that lists the current writing competitions - https://www.facebook.com/awritesite

There are thousands of writing competitions going at any one time and some are free and some you must pay to enter

– usually around $10-20. There are websites dedicated to listing writing competitions and they make a fun and lucrative way to fund your bigger writing project.

You can check my Facebook page where I keep writers updated on current competitions ...

https://www.facebook.com/awritesite

Writing competitions can be for full-length novels but, usually, they're for much shorter tomes:

- Poetry
- Short stories
- Flash fiction – usually under 1,000 words and sometimes under 500 words
- Chapbooks, which I hadn't heard of till a few days ago, and
- Short movie scripts

So, stop the car, breathe some fresh air and try new experiences along the way. It can be fun and it can look great on your CV when you're pitching to writers' agents or publishers.

How Long Should My Book Be?

... and other writing facts

Book lengths

Of course, you don't have to write a whole book. 120,000 words might just be too much for you. It might not be who you are. So, you can write shorter works. As a rough guide, the different classes of writing are:

Novel: 55,000-300,000 words
Novella: 30,000-50,000 words
Short stories: 1,500-3,000 words
Flash fiction: Usually under 1,000 words

Therefore, if you like writing short stories, you could join a writing group and they, typically, publish a compilation book every so often. Some do this every year. So you can have your short story (or stories) featured there. The same with any poetry you write - you can combine with others and produce a compilation book of poetry.

There are no rules or limits on your story length. For example, I have written:
- A novel of 110,000 words - *The Last Stand Down*.
- 2 novelettes of around 30,000 words - *Gerald the Great of Gorokoland* and *Circles of Gold*
- A book of 97 97-word stories - *97 SMILES*
- A book of 53 53-word stories - *53 SMILES*

- Several non-fiction books and around 500 short stories that pop up everywhere - in magazines, compilation books and my own books of short stories.

There is no need to feel the burden of a huge production of over 100,000 words - create your own genre and/or word-length type of book.

Fonts

A font is the style of the type - **Arial, Verdana,** Courier, Times Roman and so on. This book is in Roman Times, the most common font for newspapers and books, for a very good reason, which is:

The *London Times*, one of the oldest newspapers and, apparently, the publication that has produced more words than any other, has done numerous surveys on reader speed and comprehension - they wanted to improve their readers' reading experience and absorption of stories in the newspaper. They found that, when they adapted the original Roman font to what they called their own brand of it - Times Roman - then reader speed (with equal comprehension) was 24% faster than a font with no serif.

The serif is the little piece at the end of each letter. You will notice that there are no serifs on **Arial** and **Verdana** (what we call sans[1] serif fonts) and there are on Courier and Times Roman.

There is a current fashion to use sans serif fonts. However, I'd suggest that you use Times Roman for your text as publishers and readers prefer it ... which is why that font is the most favoured for mass-market typing.

---

1 *Sans*, from the French, meaning *without*.

Story Structure and Characters

Which parts of the story comes first, second and so on?

I haven't covered the story structure or characterisation in this book, so far, as the most important thing is to get words down on paper ... and having that as a consistent discipline in your life. Few writers have their first draft published ... actually, I'd venture to suggest that NO writers have had their first draft published!

If I've encouraged you to start a regular writing regime, my job is done with this book - getting enough words on paper for you to become discerning about them is a huge step forward. Congratulate yourself!

So, having written quite a few words, realised the most of the first 100,000 are absolute rubbish, written a few more, scrapped a few more and decided that the assembly before you, now, is a credible heap, you may want to start shaping it into something amazing ... if it's not already amazing!

Firstly, remember that novels are not diaries. They do not start at the beginning and move, chronologically, through to the end. The same with non-fiction. You may, of course, have a particular process that readers must go through to repair their car, improve their relationship or build their spaceship. However, we're not talking about manuals, here - we're talking about writing that people actually *want* to read! The linear process may not be best to start with.

Non-fiction, like *The Power of Now*, *The Moon is a Balloon* or *The Five Love Languages*, have a process or a chronology and that doesn't start with the first word. The first few words need to capture the readers' attention and encourage them to keep reading. After all, they have busy lives and lots of other things they could be doing - and other books they could be reading - so bring them into your story, fiction or non-fiction, with all the guile you can muster.

The start
There's an exercise, ahead[2], about your ONE BIG THING. Never forget the one big thing and, if you can start your book with it, in some way, it frames and sculpts the rest of the book.

The first few sentences have to stun and intrigue your readers. This is not the place for description. Description comes later.

So, here, at the start, there needs to be action - the herione is hanging from a cliff with the snaffle dragon breathing fire down on her ... or whatever is going on. You can describe the grey granite of the cliff, the dragon's purple scales and the heroine's blonde, curly hair a few pages later. Right now, there needs to be action or something intriguing that draws the reader in.

Description doesn't draw people in - let it be a few pages further on. Obviously, you have to use some description but, as a general rule, make description no more than 20% in the first few pages. Get the story moving and you can slow the pace later, with description. We'll cover pace in the next section.

Also, modern stories are lighter on description than, say, Jane Austen's or Charles Dickens' novels. Many modern novels don't completely describe many of the characters. Some may mention her bad breath, his annoying habit of flicking a curl

---

2 See the chapter, *What Is The Point of My Story?*

back or her tendency to bump into things. They may not tell you their height, hair colour, eye colour, race, clothes and, in a way, it can be good to make the reader work for it - giving them freedom to make their own picture of the characters and/or the scenery. And, in a way, does it matter if the reader has a different picture in their heads than you do? Obviously, if some part of a charater's appearance (or the scenery) is crucial to the story, include it. If it's not crucial, think again if it is really needed.

Middle

Within your life and every other story, there have been ups and downs, tension and peace, happy and sad. This, in a way, is what writers refer to as *pace* and NLP people might describe as a change of state.

Think about a wave and, in the first page, the wave is about to crash onto you - high excitement or something to capture the reader's attention. Hook them in at the start and, after that, imagine the wave rising and falling. There needs to be tension and then, shall we say, looseness, where the wave recedes in readiness for it's next onslaught on the hapless sand.

For example, many novels scatter their descriptions of particular characters throughout the book. On the second page it might be about their gnarly fingers. On page five it might mention their hairy legs and squinty eyes. It might not be till page twenty that we find out the character is from Ethiopia. We don't have to tell the reader everything about a character when they first meet them.

Think of description as the receding wave and action as the advancing wave. It's like a well structured dance between forward and backward, upbeat and slow beat.

Even in thriller novels, the reader needs to take a breath, so to speak, where the fast, furious action is interspersed with description and back-story, which is story before the current event. We need back-story and we need description and just be aware of where it is in the flow (pace) of your story.

End

Short stories, in particular, need to have a surprising or unexpected ending. That, in a way, is the essence of the short story - a story with a twist in its tail. Without that twist or surprise, your short story is likely to fall flat.

Novels, too, need to have a well thought-out ending. Thrillers and romance novels typically start with a lots of action (humorous action in many romances) and then things get complicated. Then, near the end, things become impossible and the hero is about to be defeated or the boy seems unlikely to get the girl. The tension rises as we smell defeat in the air ... then, right at the end, there's a twist, a surprise, and the hero is saved or the couple finally get it together.

Usually, it is unwise to reveal the ending too soon. Don't make it obvious until you really need to. Keep readers thinking and guessing. After all, reading is perceived as a passive activity but, in reality, the more the reader has to work or use their mental faculties, the more engaged they will be in the story. After all, manuals tell you the end even before you start ... and you know how engaging they are!

So, yes, the content of your story - what it's about - needs to be interesting but, equally important, is the way you spread the butter over the toast, so to speak. The same story can be told uin countless ways so make sure you step back from the detail and observe the flow (or pace) of information being fed to the reader. Do they need to take a breath and a slower pace? Do they need a slap about the chops and be woken up after a slow scene?

Being aware of pace can make or break your story - fiction or non-fiction.

FOR PLANNERS

So you're a planner. Pantsers don't understand you, your need of structure, for frameworks, for certainty and all that premeditated stuff. But you understand this and that's okay.

So, here we go. This is your moment. Just complete the forms in the order given and you'll see your beautiful creation rise from the order that follows.

For Pantsers

If you're a pantser, I urge you to complete the forms as well. It will be difficult, like pushing butter up a porcupine's bum with a hot needle. It will go right against your nature but I challenge you to stop the flow of your beautiful words, for a moment, and obey some rules.

For everyone

There are several benefits to completing the following forms:

1. It will help you avoid writer's block. With a firm, written plan of where your story is going and (perhaps) ending, you're creating a life-line to tow you into the future, to tow you to the end of your book.

2. It can save you a lot of time, taking out diversions which you'll later delete as they didn't relate to your story.

3. It will help you create elevator speeches, synopses and story outlines; all necessary when approaching writers agents and/or publishers. This will also help when designing the cover

blurb, when writing introductions inside your book and for writing about your book on your website and other social media venues … it's stuff you have to do, anyway, so why not do it now and have the benefit from the start!

For more courses, resources and forces to help you write your book use your phone to scan this QR Code - you'll be taken to my website at https://writethatbooknow.com

Why Are You Writing This book?

What bugs you?

Maybe you just love the process of writing and don't really care what effect your words have ... but, no, you're kidding yourself if you think that. Yes, you might enjoy writing but let's not pretend, huh! Everyone wants to make an impact on the world, to leave a unique footprint that isn't washed away by the tides of time. A vain wish, to be sure, but a real one in the heart of every human.

A memoir for your children is an obvious example of the footprint-leaving thing.

A business book to promote your business and/or to help your clients/customers is another.

If it's a non-fiction book, it's likely that your interest stems from something good or bad that happened to you previously.

If it's a novel, a made-up story, there's still a part of you in it.

Many people write fiction or non-fiction as therapy – there's some life trauma you can release through words on paper. Also, you're likely to want to help people deal with whatever you've gone through.

Eddy Izzard, famous English comedian who has run over 40 marathons, says everything he has done is because his mother died early in his life. He's tried to fill the hole left by her absence with constant and sometimes risky activity.

- What is it that annoys you about the world?

- What injustice do you feel needs to be righted?
- What trauma/challenge have you faced and overcome … or not overcome but you're determined to help others with it?
- What sector of society (or group of people) do you feel the most empathy and/or sympathy for?
- What part of the world needs help? Maybe it's not people but the environment, animals, economic systems, political systems, technology, corporate greed … the list goes on.

For writing to touch people's hearts, it must touch yours. And, vice versa - if it touches your heart, it will touch someone else's.

So, I'm suggesting that you can write about absolutely anything you like. It doesn't have to be a passion of yours. However, words will come easier and readers will arrive quicker if it's from that deep place in your soul. And, if you're struggling with what to write about, ask yourself the previous questions - your answer will come from one of them.

Why Are You Writing This book?

Where have you been?

Write down the list of your:
- Qualifications
- Jobs
- The occupations you wished you had done
- Things to did and experienced as a child – good and bad
- What you excelled at in school … and what you wanted to excel in
- Influential people (both annoying and inspiring) you have met
- Charities you've helped in
- Your past and current interests, hobbies, sports or groups you're in
- The things people do that inspire you or wish you could do

If you've been there and done it - a place, job, experience, life situation - then you don't have to do so much research and your descriptions will be more vivid.

It is no surprise that many successful authors write about their past experience/qualifications:
- John Grisham was a corporate lawyer so writes about corporate law.
- Jeffrey Archer was a politician so writes about political intrigue.

- Ken Kesey (*One Flew Over The Cuckoos Nest*) was a voluntary participant in CIA psych tests, unwittingly dosed with LSD.
- Herman Melville (*Moby Dick*) was employed as a cabin boy on a cruise liner.
- John Green worked as a chaplain at a children's hospital as part of the discernment process, and the stories of the people he met there eventually inspired his book *The Fault in Our Stars*.
- For 10 years, Rainbow Rowell wrote for the Omaha-World Herald, so it's no surprise that her novel *Attachments* so perfectly captures the life of newspaper employees.
- Agatha Christie was an apothecaries' assistant - helpful for her murder mysteries.

Most of us think our lives are ordinary and uninteresting. They may be to us as we're in them every single day. However, to an outsider, our lives may seem romantic, exciting and fascinating. So, please do not diminish the experiences you've had so far - they could be just what others want to read about.

Obviously, you don't have to write about what you know - science fiction writers don't! - but it can certainly help.

Why This Book?

Matching passions with experiences

It's obvious that your most powerful writing comes from your deepest passion or grievance. Similarly, the easiest subjects to write on are the ones you've experienced, lived through and trained for – you've already done the research!

Match what bugs you with what you've been through and you may (or may not) be surprised at the matching that occurs.

What bugs you?	Experiences and trainings
The stifling of spirit	An abusive father
Financial abundance, security and freedom	Bankrupt parents
Political intrigue	A political career

WHAT IS THE POINT OF YOUR STORY?

The ONE BIG THING

Now that you've become a little clearer on your motivation(s) for writing this story – fiction or non-fiction – what is the point of your story? Obviously, a non-fiction book – on business, health, the environment, travel, wine, underwater knitting or whatever – has a specific reason to exist; to inform, to help and (possibly) to bring in new customers.

Non-fiction
However clear your intention is, it's likely you have a list of remedies/techniques/solutions for your non-fiction clients. Despite that, it is helpful to find ONE BIG THING that you're telling your readers … the ONE BIG THING that all your other ideas and solution hang from.

For example, you may have a book to help people start their own business – business structure, registering for tax, marketing ideas, staffing issues, legal restraints, dealing with customers, social media and so on. However, within all those separate issues, there may be ONE BIG THING you want to focus on. It may be:
- Find the courage (an emotional approach)
- How to avoid tax (a middle digit up at the system)

- A step by step book (a logical, systematic approach)

There are many ways to tell the same story so dig back into the previous table – matching passions with experiences – and you might see where you're coming from, so to speak.

Fiction

Okay, I know you're possibly not an evangelist, wanting to set the world on fire. If you are, that's fine, too. If you are or you're not, think about the previous table – matching passions with experience – and you may find ONE BIG THING that you want to tell the world, through the medium of fiction.

- Maybe you just want to tell a darned good yarn, give people a humorous, thrilling, impelling and/or inspiring time away from their wretched little world while they bury themselves in your story.
- Maybe there's some social issue – domestic violence, the environment, discrimination, conspiracies, injustice – you'd like to air out on your washing line of a story.
- Maybe there's something closer to home – family history, the importance of family/friends, an inspiring person who changed your life in some way, the importance of respect, connection or honesty.
- Maybe you want to make people think – conspiracies, mysteries, possible futures, fantasy.
- Maybe, maybe, maybe ... there's lots of good, bad, ugly and possible reasons for taking on the massive task of writing a book and pushing it (and yourself) out into the public realm.

Ordering Thoughts And Emotions

Unjumbling the jumble

As you sit down with a heart full of writing desire but a mind empty of words, stop a moment. Look around. Breathe. Smile. Then, whether it is a 150,000-word novel or a 1,000-word flash fiction, follow this simple, five-step process:

Column 1: Identify the Writing Situation or Event
Here you just write down the physical facts right now. For example, that it is time to do your writing and you are at your desk with your laptop open and ready for a writing session. Are you at home, in a café, at work or somewhere else? Is it quiet or noisy? Are you safely alone or are you likely to be interrupted?

Column 2: Negative Emotions
In this column, write down the emotions you are feeling and give them a rating of intensity expressed as a percentage. For example, anxiety 40%, anger 20%, self-doubt 30%, excitement 10% and so on.

Column 3: Self-Cherishing, Irrational Thoughts
Next you write a numbered list of your irrational thoughts about your writing. For example:

- I'm hopeless at turning up to write regularly.
- There's no point in doing my writing because it won't be any good, however hard I try.
- I'm faking it and don't really know much about my subject.
- I wish I could write with more emotion, humour or whatever ... but I can't.

Just write down whatever negative thoughts come to mind.

Column 4: Question yourself

Ask yourself if the negative response is realy, really true:

Negative response	Questioning
I'm hopeless at turning up to write regularly.	Really? I actually made it today and I can just program my alarm to ensure I'm here every day, at the right time. It's worth trying, anyway.
I'm faking it and don't really know much about my subject.	True. I do know a bit but I have Google and I know three people I can talk to about this. So, I may not know everything but I can research.
No one will want to read about this subject	Actually, I don't know that so it's not true.
I never finish what I start - this is a waste of time.	Hang on, I started that qualification and finished it. I started on that home renovation project and I completed it. Mmm, maybe it's not true!

Column 4: Rational and Other-Cherishing Responses

In this column you turn your attention to identifying the distortion in your negative thinking and replace your defeating (negative) emotions with enhancing beliefs for your writing. You might write something like: "How can I know before the event that my writing isn't going to be any good? Instead of assuming the worst, why not just make a start, keep an open mind, focus on getting into a creative flow … and just see how it goes …"

Column 5: Negative Emotions (After)
Finally, rewrite the emotions from column 2 and give them a new rating after having transformed your thoughts and feelings in column 4. So, for example, "anxiety" may be down to 10% and "anger" reduced to 2%. In the meantime excitement, peace, clarity, confidence and hope may have gone up.

For a workbook to help you complete these exercises, use your phone to scan this QR Code - you'll be taken to my website at https://writethatbooknow.com

Words Are But Symbols of Symbols

I don't know how to explain intangible things.

A writer's lot is not a happy one ... well, it's a happy one but not always an easy one. As *A Course in Miracles* says, words are but symbols of symbols and someone else said a picture is worth a thousand words. So, to describe anything can be a lovely and/or difficult challenge – especially things which aren't solid, tangible and visible. I'll give you an example:

In 2015 Anna and I went to the Global Retreat centre, near Oxford, for a two-day Raja Meditation retreat. As part of the experience, we were given four questions and asked to write whatever answers arose from them. Now, I ask you – how do you describe God, heaven or your true spiritual nature?

Here are the questions and the answers that sprang from me:

1. What is soul? Spirit? Consciousness?
The experience or knowing of God – the deep nothingness from which arises all potential, all creation. The fecund presence of openness and expansion. The beingness of the void.

2. How does it feel?
Empty and full, sweet and simple, like a silent smile.

3. What is silence?
The unutterable voice of creativity, the smell of a rainbow, an unopened seed of potentiality.

4. What does "knowing me" mean?
Loosening the garments of labels and judgements of The World to reveal the utter endlessness and depth from which I sprang. Knowing I am nothing but the silent, empty potential of all that is, all that can ever be. Stripped of the bandage and bondage of The World, Me is the wind of change and the tree of stillness, rooted in God and growing towards Godliness. Me is nothing. Me isn't. Me is divinity within the folds of an endless movement towards a point of light. Me is.

They meant something to me and they still do – a deep and profound meaning. However, do they mean anything to you?

The strange thing with intangibles is that they are both hard to describe but they're a fun challenge. Also, because they do not "exist", we have to use symbolism and unusual words and phrases to describe them. Some people find this fun and some do not like it. However, before you write yourself off as incapable of describing intangibles, try the exercise below and watch what happens. You may have a renewed respect for your writing ability. Try it now with ...

- Knowing something in your heart that you can't explain to others or that others will disagree with. How do you describe that knowing?
- How do you describe Love?
- How do you describe fear, anger, anxiety or depression?
- Find some words to describe the birth of your first child, the starting of your first business or your first bicycle as a child.
- How do you describe weather that's so hot or cold that it hurts?

Philip J Bradbury

AMBIDEXTROUS WRITING

Answers to all my questions

This is used to explore various sub-personalities through two-handed writing. Your main hand is the one you usually use for writing – if you're right handed, your main hand is your right hand and your other hand is your left. Your main hand is the "facilitator" (question) and your other hand is the "client" (answer).

Create two columns on paper and your right hand writes in the right column and your left hand in the left column ... or vice versa if you are left handed.

Writre questions with your main (facilitator) hand and write answers with your other (client) hand. Your client will probably be annoyingly ackward and write in a scrawl but this doesn't matter, just let the writing flow – it is the message that's important.

When you write a question with your main hand, the first thought (response) is the correct one to write with your other hand. Sometimes the answers may seem illogical, silly or illelevant but just put down what first comes to mind. Sometimes the answers may seem like silly "mind chatter" and sometimes they may be very profound and surprisingly helpful. Just keep asking and responding, without judgement, and let each first thought (answer) flow onto the paper.

Don't try to consciously guide or demand a particular

response. If there is no response to a particular question, you may be trying too hard – this is one of those nice jobs in life where the lazier you are, the better it gets done. Just relax your body and mind, become a hollow bamboo through which the whispers of your subconscious speak, and try again.

If still no response arrives or you are getting frustrated, write that down as a response (e.g. "No response", "I'm getting frustrated", "Stupid mind, can't think!" or whatever) and ask the next question. Keep the process moving. That you are stuck or frustrated are, in fact, valid answers and can tell you much, if looked at later, with all the other responses you had.

As an example, this is an exercise I did. This paper's not wide enough to show the 2 columns that I used but you can see the process at work.

Q: What is my main writing theme, for all my writing?
A: Give people hope.
Q: How do I do that - fiction or non-fiction?
A: Both, as well as teaching.
Q: That's not that helpful. Okay, what should I be writing today?
A: Non-fiction. Get this course finished. Stop procrastinating!
Q: How will I know I have finished this book - there is an unending number of things I can write about.
A: Not a novel. Short and sweet and you'll know when you stop needing to ask that question.
Q: How will I know?
A: There will be a definite knowing. Trust!
Q: Grr! Okay, what colour should the cover be?
A: White.
Q: Why white?
A: La tabla rusa - the blank slate. It will represent the empty page we face each day.
Q: Thank you.

About the Author

In New Zealand I experienced life as an accountant, credit manager, company director, shepherd, scrub-cutter, tree pruner, freezing worker, plastics factory worker, saxophonist, army driver, tour bus driver, stage and television actor and singer, builder, lecturer, facilitator for men's groups, reporter, columnist, magazine editor, publisher, writer ...

In South Africa as an AIDS workshop co-facilitator ...

In the Australian bush as a barman, horse and camel trekker and stock-whip teacher ...

In England as a contract accountant, corporate trainer, estate manager, lecturer, singer/songwriter, website editor/writer and freelance writer ...

Now that I'm back in Australia, house renovating, teaching and writing, I'm wondering what's next!

The constant for me is *A Course in Miracles*, a psychological life-style course in forgiveness. Through it I have found the peace I had always been searching for - the journey to where we have always been.

Social media

Website: www.philipjbradbury.com
Wordpress blogs:
   https://flashfictionfanatic.wordpress.com/
   https://pjbradbury.wordpress.com/
Amazon: amzn.to/25X0CLb
Facebook:
   https://www.facebook.com/AuthorPhilipJBradbury/
Linked In - http://bit.ly/2aTzZMS
Smashwords: http://bit.ly/2aNjkic
Twitter: https://twitter.com/PhilipJBradbury

www.ingramcontent.com/pod-product-compliance
Lightning Source LLC
Chambersburg PA
CBHW050317010526
44107CB00055B/2285